Lowlife

Lowlife

LIFE IN PRISON WITH DRUG DEALERS, GUN RUNNERS AND MURDERERS

SIMON EDDISBURY

JOHN BLAKE

Published by John Blake Publishing Ltd,
3 Bramber Court, 2 Bramber Road,
London W14 9PB, England

www.johnblakepublishing.co.uk

First published in paperback in 2010

ISBN: 9781844549603

British Library Cataloguing-in-Publication Data:

A catalogue record for this book is available from the British Library.

Design by www.envydesign.co.uk

Printed and bound by CPI Group (UK) Ltd, Croydon, CR0 4YY

3 5 7 9 10 8 6 4 2

Papers used by John Blake Publishing are natural, recyclable products made
from wood grown in sustainable forests. The manufacturing processes
conform to the environmental regulations of the country of origin.

Dedicated to good people who do bad things.

Although I was living the low life during my time locked up, that's not to say that the people I met were lowlives. To everyone behind the prison walls – keep your head up and remember that your day will come. I'd like to thank my mum and dad for putting up with me and everyone who wrote to me for making my time inside more bearable. Without you, this would never have been possible.

CONTENTS

INTRODUCTION

On 7 August 2008 I was arrested for the offence of selling Class A drugs to an undercover police officer. I had sold three £10 bags of MDMA, that being the active chemical in ecstasy. I was by no means a career criminal and had been naïvely dabbling in crime in order to pay off my student loan. As I sat cuffed up in the back of the police car I began to reflect upon the severity of my situation. I was almost certainly heading to prison. The car pulled up at the police station and my heart began to race. I had been very stupid and was now about to face the consequences.

After an eight-hour stint in the holding cells followed by extensive interrogation, I was finally released on bail to attend court in a few months' time. This was to be several months of intense worry. Being university-educated and thoroughly middle-class, and having had no previous dealings with the police or the legal system, I had no idea what to expect. The prospect of going to jail and living the next few years of my life among murderers, rapists and paedophiles was quite frankly terrifying. I spent my spare time up until the court case gathering character references, planning my defence and generally doing everything in my power to try to avoid a custodial sentence. Finally the day of reckoning came, and I got one anyway. Two and a half years, to be precise.

As I sat in yet another holding cell waiting to be transported to the prison I felt rightfully wounded. A few bags of brown crystalline powder had cost me my comfort, my safety and my peace of mind for the foreseeable future. The next few years were going to be extremely difficult, but I would get through them, I told myself. There had to be something positive that could come from all of this. What were the benefits of going to jail? It would be an experience, I suppose. Probably not a particularly good one but an experience nonetheless. I could spend my time finding out what makes the criminal mind tick. I had always been interested in crime and why people choose to become involved in it. This was my chance to find out first-hand. This could be my focus throughout my sentence – finding out as much as I could about why the other prisoners had ended up there in the first place. It might help to take my mind off the dismal surroundings and poor company. My mind was made up – I was going to make something of my time behind bars and ask a hell of a lot of questions.

What you are about to read is the result of unfortunate circumstances and an inquisitive mind. During my sentence I spoke to more than 50 different offenders, from shoplifters to armed robbers and everything in between. I uncovered a particularly dark and seedy world inhabited by people intent on taking what doesn't belong to them, whatever the cost. True-crime books tend to portray criminals as Robin Hood-type characters – lovable rogues who take from society as a whole to give back to their deprived communities. Unfortunately, this is not how real criminals are. While some of them are good people driven to crime through difficult circumstances, there are equally many who are completely amoral and lead very dark lives indeed. Crack, smack, guns, knives, torture and mutilation are all commonplace. It was time for my highlife of hedonistic excess to come to an end. I was about to live the low life. Names have been changed to protect the guilty.

CHAPTER 1

BOLTY

One of the first professional criminals I spoke to in depth during my time behind bars was a guy called Bolty. Word had spread that I was looking to write a book and he was keen to be in it. There is a common misconception that talking about your crime in prison is taboo. This could not be further from the truth: criminals love to talk. If they had their way they would tell you about their crimes all day every day, and Bolty was no exception. He was surprisingly friendly and approachable for an armed robber, and all too willing to fill me in on every last detail of his lengthy criminal history.

Bolty looked like your typical sink-estate resident. His arms were lined with tattoos, as were those of the majority of the other inmates, and he had the look of a man who, although currently relaxed and sociable, could easily turn violent. He came from a deprived inner-city area of Hull infamous for drugs and prostitution, and he had been involved in crime from a very young age. At just 10 years old he had started smoking weed and by the time he was 11 he had been kicked out of school for starting a blazing inferno while trying to put out a joint in the wastepaper bin.

This didn't bother Bolty in the slightest – he'd had a dislike of authority from day one and education had never really been his thing. Instead he chose to spend his time shoplifting and stealing motorbikes, riding them triumphantly around his estate to show off to his peers. At this point he was involved in crime purely for recreational purposes. He liked the buzz he got from taking something that wasn't his and the feeling of power that it gave him. At age 11 most children wouldn't even know what weed was and would certainly have no idea how to drive a motorcycle. He was a problem child. A product of the harsh surroundings in which he was raised – forced to grow up too quickly.

After a prolific spate of bike thefts Bolty was labelled uncontrollable and placed in a special unit for disruptive children. He was now 13 – a teenager and no longer a child. What may have been excused in the past was now inexcusable. The theory was that, if he was removed from the familiar surroundings of his estate, it might break him out of the cycle of crime and antisocial behaviour. He was taken to a small village in rural Pembrokeshire to live among other troubled teenagers from similar backgrounds. Unfortunately, he was the most troubled of the bunch and terrorised the entire village. Anything that wasn't nailed down he took.

'I must have robbed every shop in the village at some point,' Bolty grinned, clearly revelling in the chaos he had caused in a place that had probably never been exposed to a delinquent of his magnitude. If he had taken one or two items here and there he might have avoided detection, but one thing that characterises thieves is their love of excess. He wanted everything it was humanly possible to steal, and as far as he was concerned it was all easy pickings. 'The first time I got caught I robbed a gas gun at this shooting range they took us to,' he told me. A sign of things to come, given his future predilection for firearms. 'I got caught but I was already locked up, so what could they really do?' This was a fairly petty offence and one that could be swept under the rug. What was to follow would take things up a level and help cement his path to becoming a professional crook.

Unlike prison or young offenders' institutions, the home in which Bolty was placed was fairly relaxed and family members were allowed to come and go as they pleased, taking their felonious offspring on outings and shopping sprees in a vain attempt to pacify their lust for crime. It was one such outing that enabled him to steal ten grand's worth of jewellery and secure himself a lifetime ban from Pembrokeshire. Despite his troubled ways his mum still loved him and, to show him this, she had made the six-hour journey from Hull to take him to buy a gold ring in one of the local shops. But a single item of gold was not enough to quench his magpie-like thirst for shiny objects, and Bolty had ideas of his own. While his mum was browsing the rings and chatting to

the shop assistant he was sneaking into the backroom to
fill his pockets with everything he could get his hands
on. What he failed to notice was that the security camera
was pointing straight at him. He was promptly arrested
and all other outings of this nature were cut short.

Every mother has her limits and no one takes the
decision to put their teenage son into a care home lightly,
but there was clearly no other option left. It was either
that or live with a kleptomaniac who would steal
anything and everything despite only just having come
back from Pembrokeshire, where he was supposed to
have been rehabilitated. Had Mrs Bolt known what the
average care home was like, she might have thought
twice. Care homes are not nice places. Many of the
children have emotional and behavioural problems and
drugs and alcohol are rife. If she'd had the gift of foresight
she might have acted differently, but, as it stood, she
didn't know what else to do, so, again, Bolty was passed
into the hands of the system.

'That's when I first started selling weed,' Bolty told me.
'At first it was just to get enough for a smoke and a few
beers but then I realised how much money I could make.'
This was the first step in his progression from recreational
felon to full-time career criminal. He was now profiting
from his crime as opposed to doing it purely for the rush.
As a good percentage of the other residents at the home
smoked weed, he could serve the majority of his customers
without even leaving the house. It was the perfect crime of
convenience. Soon enough he was selling to teenagers and
adults alike and making a healthy income.

It was rather naïve to think that someone who was so heavily involved in crime at such a young age could be put right by a spell in a care home. If his own mother had failed to tame his wild ways, why would a government-employed care worker be any different? Time and time again Bolty rebelled. Any rules or regulations imposed upon him were completely disregarded and he became a thorn in the side of the social services. Eventually his behaviour was deemed unmanageable and he was placed in a secure unit – the third institution he had been shifted to within a single year.

A secure unit is basically a prison for those under the age of 15. They are usually reserved as a last resort, as it is not the norm to lock up children of this age for anything short of a serious offence. 'It didn't faze me, though,' Bolty stated matter-of-factly, his face showing no emotions to suggest otherwise. 'It was just like being in another care home.' For all intents and purposes one institution was very much the same as another. Everywhere he was placed followed a familiar pattern – they were all full of feral children from deprived inner-city areas who in many cases yearned for what they could not have. He fitted in nicely and even went as far as to say he enjoyed his first taste of true incarceration.

A lot can change over a nine-month period and those who have been locked up can often find a different world awaiting them on their release. In this particular case it was the drugs that had changed. Until this point Bolty had really encountered only marijuana, but, now that his peer group were a little bit older, they had moved onto the harder stuff. Cocaine and Valium were the order of the day. Unlike the weed, these were highly addictive drugs and many had developed a dependency. Rather than spend the odd tenner here and there on a joint, people would now plough everything they earned into coke. The potential for making a lot of money in a short period of time was irresistible. At 14 years of age the young entrepreneur's main source of income quickly became Class A drugs.

Despite being a mere novice, Bolty was soon earning in excess of a thousand pounds a week. The problem was that he was spending it all on stupid things. One of the things I came to realise from my time in prison is that criminals don't seem to know how to budget. They become accustomed to incredibly lavish lifestyles and it is not uncommon for them to spend at least a thousand pounds a week on clothes. This leaves them constantly craving more money. It was for this reason that selling drugs was no longer enough. In order to make big money Bolty would have to take what everyone else had made as well.

The act of robbing a drug dealer – or any other criminal – is known in such circles as 'taxing' (see Glossary). It is a risky business, as many dealers arm themselves in anticipation of such an eventuality. However, at 15 years of age Bolty felt he was ready for the challenge. Armed with a baseball bat, he took it upon himself to burst into a small-time crack and heroin dealer's house in the middle of the night and take him for all he had. He came away with £500 in cash and £2,000 worth of crack and smack. This was meagre pickings – he could have earned the same amount from burgling a house. To make matters worse, his victim unexpectedly broke one of the biggest taboos in the book and went to the police, mentioning only the theft of the money and leaving out all references to the stolen drugs. What had taken place was legally classed as aggravated burglary, carrying a maximum sentence of life in prison. Things had gone horribly wrong.

Twelve months. Bolty could have got a lot longer, so, all things considered, this was not a bad result. He had been in so many institutions already, so a young offenders' was just another one to add to the collection. It was nothing new to him whatsoever and did nothing to stop him from committing future crimes. 'I can't say I was at all afraid of going back,' he told me. Such institutions acted as little deterrent when there was so much to be gained from the proceeds of his crimes.

A year passed and things had changed yet again on the streets of Hull. Crack and smack were the new big thing and all his friends were now selling them. Cocaine and Valium may be addictive but there are people who would kill their own mothers to get hold of crack or heroin, so custom was in constant supply. Not one to miss out on a graft, Bolty was straight on it and immediately invested in large amounts of both substances. Or should I say *allegedly* invested, as he made it very clear what he had been doing without directly saying anything that could have incriminated himself?

The amount to be earned from selling crack and smack

7

was double that from selling coke and Valium. Business was booming and Hull was now experiencing a crack epidemic, with areas like Gipsyville, Orchard Park and Bransholme bearing the brunt of it. This brought with it a wave of new social problems, including disease, child abuse and prostitution. Whereas most cocaine users lived relatively normal lives and worked nine-to-five jobs, those unlucky enough to have got themselves hooked on crack and heroin thought about nothing else and would stop at nothing to get their daily fix. They were, as one inmate had put it, 'the scum of the earth'.

'Some of my best customers were in the red-light district on Porter Street,' Bolty stated bluntly, seemingly with no regard for the bleak situation these 'customers' had been placed in by their addiction. Of course, he didn't specifically say that they had been buying drugs – when I asked him what he had been selling to them he just laughed. Clearly anyone was fair game and he had failed to make the connection that anybody desperate enough to sell their body to fund a drug habit was in a very low place indeed. But then again most smackheads were willing to do whatever it took: robbing old grannies, burgling houses on Christmas Eve, selling the clothes off their backs – these were all things I heard being talked about.

At 16 it was time for Bolty to get his first gun. 'How did you know where to get it from?' I asked, naïve enough to assume that firearms were still a rarity on the streets of Britain. During my sentence I was to learn that guns are rife in every town in England and that the worst parts of every city are infested with assault rifles, MAC-10s and even hand grenades. Bolty just laughed. 'I live in a rough place,' he told me. 'Guns are everywhere.' It was funny how Hull had never been in the media for gun crime. I had always assumed that the newspapers presented a sensationalised view of such things but I was soon to find out that the true extent of the problem goes far deeper than has ever been reported. Every town and city has its rough estates and these are places where the man with the biggest gun is king.

'It was a converted black Beretta,' he told me. 'In Hull we don't really use automatics. There's a few with MAC-10s, but there's no need for it really. Pistols are easier to carry. My gun of choice is the Beretta.' He talked about his gun as if it were a toy, not a weapon. 'Where people go wrong is keeping their straps in their house – I always hide mine in the drainpipe of this house on our estate.' This could have landed the innocent residents with a lengthy jail sentence. 'Better them go down for it than me,' he replied.

Bolty used his black Beretta not only for his own protection but also for robbing other dealers who were bold enough to sell on his patch. This served two purposes: first, to gain him a little extra windfall every now and again; and, second, to ensure that there were fewer rival dealers in his area who could take his customers. He would ask anyone who didn't buy off him where they got their drugs from and then bam! Their front door was coming off and he was there with a gun in their face.

The main problem with taxing was that most drug dealers were fairly cowardly when it came down to it and tended to run straight to the police. In a subculture where the only moral code that counts is 'don't grass', it is strange to think that so many people choose to break this fundamental rule. But in reality there is no honour among thieves and most villains are willing to do whatever it takes to protect their livelihood. Bolty knew this all too well. After a string of lengthy jail sentences for aggravated burglary he was beginning to realise that it wasn't really worth the effort. Finally, he came to the conclusion that, rather than tax all the local dealers, it would be more sensible to threaten them into buying their drugs from him. So he collected his trusty Beretta from the drainpipe and went to pay them all a visit. 'Of course, these are all things that a good "friend" of mine did,' he grinned.

'The problem with all of this was that it stepped on other people's toes,' he told me. This should have been fairly obvious, as the person from whom the dealers usually bought would not have been best pleased with the sudden dramatic decrease in clientele. 'This guy rang my "friend" up chatting all kinds of shit and asked him to meet him down the local pub,' he went on. 'When he sat down, he started telling him that he could either agree to give him half of whatever he made or that one of them wasn't walking out of there. My "friend" knew he was walking out of there 'cause he had his strap on him!' Despite this fact, Bolty's 'friend' had decided to err on the side of caution and told him he would need time to consider the options before him. The other dealer grudgingly agreed and they went their separate ways.

Whereas many would have caved in under the pressure, Bolty's 'friend' had remained calm and collected, and was not going to be rushed into making a rash decision. 'He thought about it and the answer was no!' For all his flaws, this guy sure had some balls. 'The bloke was obviously scared or he wouldn't have given him the option to give him half – he would have just said that he couldn't sell there.'

In jail there is an ideological divide between white criminals and black criminals. This is based on the existence of the 'straightener', an organised fight that takes place to resolve an issue. Black criminals generally seem to think such a concept is ridiculous in an age when guns and knives are so prevalent: 'I'm a nigger – I don't do straighteners. I shoot people,' one black inmate eloquently explained to me. However, as Bolty was white and Hull was a predominantly white city, he agreed to send one of his associates over to fight the dealer and settle the issue once and for all. 'He smashed him all over the place' – and that was that. What could have been a bloody turf war was settled in a single fistfight in one afternoon. It was strange to think such a system was still so binding among people who made a living from dishonesty, but reassuring that they still had aspects of restraint in their culture.

'Where I lived was smackhead central. Now that my "friend" was the biggest dealer there, he was making a lot of money from it.' If only it had been enough. The crux of the matter was that, however much he got, he still wanted more. Just as addicts will do anything for drugs, 'grafters' will often do anything for money and are driven by greed to do more and more extreme things. There was also the matter of the buzz. Selling drugs was all well and good but it lacked the sudden rush of power that could be gained from putting a gun to someone's head, so Bolty's converted black Beretta was never far from his side, despite the trouble that it would eventually cause him.

The first time the police had caught him with a firearm was during a routine stop-and-search. Fortunately for Bolty, the gun was without its firing pin and so was classed as deactivated by British law and perfectly legal. The second time he had been seen on CCTV firing off shots in a local park, or so the police had told him. He had denied it was him, and luckily for him they were unable to recover the gun and had insufficient evidence to prosecute. After a few narrow escapes, Bolty began to feel invincible. He had been caught with a gun and caught on camera firing it but he was still a free man. He could do what he wanted and there would surely be no consequences to his actions.

It was at this point that selling drugs became monotonous and thrills needed to be sought elsewhere. Gone were the days when you could hold up other villains without their going to the police, but the rush of adrenaline from taking what belonged to somebody else through sheer force of firepower was something he would sorely miss. That's when it hit him. If other criminals were likely to go to the police, there was no difference between robbing them and robbing law-abiding citizens, apart from the fact that they were more likely to be able to identify him. If he masked up and hit up shops and petrol stations, there would be a lot less chance of detection.

'My mates all had their own guns, so we put together a little firm and went on the rampage,' Bolty explained. 'We did it for the buzz more than anything.' Unfortunately for him, he managed to get himself grassed up again. 'I don't know who did it – probably someone jealous of the money we were making,' he told me with a hint of anger in his voice. It was clearly someone he had confided in who had betrayed him. 'It was after we'd done this petrol station – we only got a few hundred each!' It was small pickings and certainly not worth the lengthy jail sentence he got in return.

'Do you regret what you did?' I asked, still slightly taken aback at how blasé he appeared about putting people in potentially life-threatening situations, from which they were likely to suffer lasting mental trauma. 'Yeah, now I've had some time to think about it,' Bolty responded, his demeanour softening up a touch and showing a more human side to his character. 'This sentence has given me a lot of time to reflect.'

A key factor in this period of reflection seemed to have been a newfound spirituality he had gained in jail. Like a lot of long-term prisoners, he had chosen to convert to Buddhism during his sentence. Buddhism is the fastest-growing religion in British jails and the number of converts has risen eightfold over the past decade. The main reason for this is the meditative aspect of the faith

– it helps prisoners to cope and instils in them a sense of calm in an otherwise frantic environment.

Bolty's newly acquired Buddhist faith had affected his life in a number of profound ways. It had made him calmer and less likely to get caught up in things in the heat of the moment. It also allowed him to empathise more with his victims and to put himself in their shoes. 'I'm going straight when I get out,' he told me, 'or at the very least I'm going to tone it down a bit.' Well, at least he was being realistic. It would be difficult for him to take up an honest profession after a lifetime of robbing and stealing, but at least this was a step in the right direction. Would he ever come back to jail? 'You can never say never,' was Bolty's response, 'although I'll try my hardest not to!'

The impression Bolty left was one of a person who had been surrounded by negative influences from day one and had stood little chance of living an honest life. In a place where drugs are everywhere and temptation is always just around the corner it is difficult not to stray from the narrow path. He seemed as though he had made a lot of progress during his sentence and that maybe a long stint behind bars was what he had needed to put him on the straight and narrow. Hopefully, now that he had his newfound peace of mind, he would be able to lead a crime-free life and finally get himself back on the right track.

CHAPTER 2
MR STRAPS

One thing puzzled me about Bolty's story. Where did all these guns that were clearly so readily available come from, and who was selling them? Someone I was told could shed a little light on this was a guy known as Mr Straps, 'straps' being street slang for firearms. As well as selling pretty much every weapon under the sun, he was a bit of a jack of all trades and had dabbled in just about every type of crime. If it was illegal, the betting was that he'd most probably been there, done that and stolen the T-shirt.

Straps spoke with a strong Northern accent with hints of Jamaican patois mixed in. He was fairly softly spoken and not at all how I would have expected an arms dealer to be. He looked the part but seemed far too good-natured for his chosen profession. But first impressions can be very deceptive and he had done more than a few dark things in his time. He'd grown up in Leeds's notorious Chapeltown area, where crime was never far away. Hookers roamed the streets, teenagers delivered drugs on pedal bikes and there were local pubs where you could buy a great deal more than just beer. Sure, the city had its nice parts, but there were also endless sprawling council estates where queues of addicts lined up for their daily fixes. To be fair, the majority of the residents there lived perfectly law-abiding lives, but for those of a less reputable nature there was an underworld of criminality and opportunities waiting to be seized.

For a guy like Straps there was never any doubt as to what he would do with his life. 'From a very early age I was involved in doing "raises",' he told me, as if implying his descent into wrongdoing was of a predetermined certainty from day one. Having witnessed older gangsters walking around with gold chains and the latest designer gear, he had always known that a nine-to-five was not for him. He didn't want to be working long hours for peanuts – he wanted large rewards for small amounts of work.

'I was a wild kid.' This was the understatement of the decade. 'I stopped going to school when I was around 13 and things went downhill from there.' It was around this time that he had first got into selling drugs. 'I always preferred the idea of selling work to doing work,' he smiled, 'work' being street slang for hard drugs. 'Not going to school, I had a lot more time to run the streets, so I started dabbling in a few things. There was always plenty of cats [drug users] about and so I used to sell them crack, brown [heroin] and Es.'

Another lucrative source of income in the area was Spencer Place, the red-light district. Anyone stupid enough to travel to an area like that to visit a prostitute was putting their life in danger. The local residents were not best pleased to have so many kerb crawlers right on their doorstep and one way of dissuading them from coming back was to beat them up and rob them. 'You could make up to five grand a night,' Straps told me. 'And who's going to go to the police and tell them they were getting a prossie at the time? A lot of these people had wives and kids and a lot to lose.'

But Straps tended to target other criminals for the majority of his 'raises'. Drug dealers were the ideal prey, as they kept large amounts of cash in their houses. In order to preserve their ill-gotten gains, they were forced to avoid banking any of it for fear of a confiscation order if they were ever to get arrested. This left them extremely vulnerable. There were two methods of taking their money: burgling their houses when they weren't in or kicking the door in, putting a gun to their head and taking it by force. Obviously, the former entailed less chance of getting grassed up but it involved finding out when the house was empty and normally relied on a tip-off from one of the dealer's so-called friends. Either method would do and Straps wasn't a particularly picky man when it came to making money.

By the time he'd reached 15, grafting had become a way of life. Why go to school when you can earn as much as a High Court judge or a doctor without so much as a GCSE or doing a fraction of the work? Drugs,

17

guns and robberies were now just a part of everyday life. To go back into education would have been completely illogical. The only institution that could teach him anything worth knowing began with the initials HMP, and it was there he learned about another highly profitable avenue of criminality to explore. 'I got this connection in jail,' he told me. 'He was bringing in straps from overseas. A lot of them came from the Ukraine and them places.' This figured, as the Ukraine had been left with huge stockpiles of military weapons after the disintegration of the Soviet Union. Many of these went missing and it is estimated that the country's illegal arms exports are now greater than its legal ones, despite its being one of the world's largest legal exporters of firearms and munitions. Countries like this were a godsend to men like Straps. If it weren't for their corruption, he would be considerably less well off.

Straps's main customers were 'gang members, street people and contacts from jail'. He had a policy of selling only to those he was friendly with and would never sell a gun to anyone he even suspected might end up using it on him or one of his associates. 'Shotguns are £150, nines are £1,200, sub-machine-guns are £30,00 and then you can get a stun gun for £150 or grenades at £50 a pop.' He reeled off the prices as if he were listing the cost of groceries. 'As well as guns I was putting out bullets and accessories,' he added. 'You could get silencers, infrared sights . . . You name it, I could sell you it. I didn't make as much from it as I did from the food [drugs] but it was a nice little sideline.'

Why bother selling guns when he was already making a healthy living from putting drugs out? Sure, the drugs were bad but at least people had a choice as to whether they took them or not. No one has the option to say no to a bullet travelling at great speed towards their face. He was effectively dealing in death and what he was doing was tantamount to mass murder. He didn't seem fazed by this in the slightest and was completely unrepentant. 'People die – it's all part of the business!' I was told. 'It's not me shooting them – I just provide the tools. Although, if it comes down to it, I would have no problems putting a bullet in someone's mum or dad.' Straps was a lot more ruthless than I had imagined. 'But their mum hasn't done anything wrong to you,' I tried to reason with him. 'It's not about the mum – it's about them and putting a message across. If you've got beef, I will take it to your mum's house.'

Straps was not a nice person. He appeared to have a very warped sense of morality and was able to override his sense of right and wrong when it came to matters of money. Whereas Bolty had come across as a victim of the place in which he had grown up, Straps seemed to be a lot more cold-hearted and callous in his actions. Although he tried not to steal from those who were in a legitimate line of business, he had no qualms about selling guns to those who did. To his credit, he always treated me with kindness and respect on the wing but the fact remained that he was a peddler of misery and grief. For as little as £50 he could sell you a weapon that could take a man's life.

What I had heard shocked me. Up until this point I hadn't even known that street criminals used things like hand grenades or that they were even available in this country. Clearly, in some forgotten areas of Britain the streets were a war zone and there were people more than willing to profit from the spoils of war. There were some truly unpleasant people behind bars, but for every cold-hearted individual there was also a lost sheep. Some people were in prison because they couldn't cope in the outside world. It was the refuge of the drug-addicted, the mentally ill and the socially inept. For every weapon used on a rival, there was one that was used to self-harm.

CHAPTER 3
WAYNE

Wayne was a cutter. He was nothing out of the ordinary – a good proportion of the inmates had scars covering their wrists where they had hacked chunks out of themselves. He was lonely. His mother kept promising to write to him but that was all it was – promises. He was doing four years for stabbing a man who he claimed had threatened to rape his sister. It was a long time to serve without contact with the outside world.

'My cellmate's not making things any easier,' he told me. 'He refuses to have the light on in the cell even when it's pitch black. I'm in the dark all the time.' This was the type of issue that inmates all over the prison would argue about. It was a minor grievance but, when you are forced to live with someone 24 hours a day, the little things mount up. 'I'm reaching boiling point,' he ranted. 'I'm going to end up stabbing him.' Wayne liked to talk about stabbing. It was one of his favourite topics of conversation. He would come into my cell telling me how he wanted to stab various different people on the wing. At first it was shocking, given what he was in for, but after a while it became just more of the same.

As time went by, Wayne got himself into increasing amounts of debt. He was a Subutex addict. Subutex is supposedly used to wean people off heroin but, from what I have seen, there are more Subutex addicts in jail than there are heroin addicts (and there are a lot of heroin addicts). A lot of them have never heard of it before they come to prison and don't realise how addictive it is until it is too late. A single 8mg tablet can go for as much as £80.

'My cellmate is still pissing me off,' he told me during one of his brief journeys out of his cell. Most of his time was spent hiding behind his door for fear of attack. He owed money to some nasty people and, until he could pay them in full, his life would be in danger. 'I wanted to watch darts on TV last night and he wouldn't let me,' he went on. 'It's the only thing I watch. We're always watching his programmes.' I braced myself for the stabbing speech. 'I'm going to slice him up soon.' Right on cue. Every day it was the same thing. 'Do you want me to have a word with him?' my cellmate asked him. Wayne looked flustered. 'N-n-no!' he stammered. 'Don't tell him any of this!' He looked scared. For all his talk, he was relatively harmless. He liked to make himself out as a violent psychopath but he was fairly passive most of the time and tended to avoid confrontation.

The next time I saw Wayne, he had a huge gash across his wrists. It was deeper than the usual lattice of scars and cuts that covered them – it looked like the result of a genuine suicide attempt. According to his cellmate, he had got up during the night, grabbed a razor blade and said, 'You know what, I can't take it any more.' He was sick of living a life of crime and addiction. Above all, he was sick of the fact that his family didn't care enough to write him a letter.

After hearing what had he had done to himself, the wing manager allowed Wayne use the office phone to ring his mother. There had already been one suicide in the prison – an inmate had hung himself within days of arrival after finding out that his girlfriend had cheated on him. They didn't want another death on their hands. His mother promised that she would write to him and apologised for the lack of letters. He told her that he was sorry for scaring her and they said their goodbyes.

Over the next few days, Wayne began to look a little perkier. He had some colour in his cheeks and was even leaving his cell door unlocked from time to time. This would have been a positive step, had he not owed half of the prison drug money. As it was, it was not a wise move. Drug dealers are generally not very sympathetic people. They didn't care that he had tried to kill himself. All they cared about was the fact that he owed them for the Subutex that he had bought off them.

Just as he was beginning to leave his cell and socialise with the other inmates, Wayne was given a violent reminder of his unpaid debts. He was sitting in his cell reading a book when the door was flung open, knocking him sideways off his chair. It was Psycho Baz – a Subutex addict renowned for his fiery temper. 'You owe Trev six packs of burn,' he snarled. ('Burn' is jail slang for rolling tobacco. It is the main currency in most British jails.) 'You can either pay up or I'll smash you.'

Wayne was terrified. Baz had a reputation for using weapons. A few weeks earlier, he had been called into another inmate's cell for a straightener. The minute the door was closed, he took out a tin of tuna, put it in a sock and beat his opponent senseless with it. He wasn't one to fight fair. 'I can pay it next week,' Wayne stammered. Before he could finish his sentence, Baz had kicked him hard in the side of the head. 'You'd better or you'll get more of the same.'

Later that day, Baz was behind me in the lunch queue. I took the opportunity to find out why he was collecting other people's debts for them. 'Wayne's got enough problems,' I told him. 'What did you do that to him for? It's not as if he owes you.' He grinned. 'Trev gave me an eight-mil [8mg Subutex tablet] to do it.' Trev was a well-known dealer from over on E Unit. 'It's nothing personal,' he went on. 'I did enjoy it, though. He screamed like a girl. If he doesn't pay up soon he'll get more of the same.'

Wayne had got himself into a sticky situation. There was no way that he would be able to pay off his debts. His mum had promised to send him some money but it hadn't arrived – nor had her letter. He was in a bad way. He had another three years left on his sentence and things weren't looking up. 'I woulda stabbed him,' he told me in an attempt to justify taking a kicking. 'But if I'd have started then I couldn't have stopped myself from killing him. I'm like that when I get going.' I rolled my eyes and looked away. Stabbing seemed to be his answer to everything, but he had let another inmate kick him in the head and done nothing about it.

That night, my sleep was disturbed by the hum of the emergency buzzer and the heavy footsteps of prison guards running towards Wayne's cell. I feared the worst. Maybe he had killed himself. He was depressed at the best of times and now that he had a bounty on his head he was at rock bottom. I tried my best to sleep through the commotion. After all, we were in jail: life was cheaper than it was on the outside.

The next morning, I went straight over to Wayne's cell to see if he was all right. He wasn't there. His cellmate was sat on the bed looking wide-eyed and shell-shocked. 'What happened?' I asked him. He pulled up his T-shirt to reveal nine stitches holding together a gash across his chest. Wayne had finally done what he'd talked about so many times. He'd slashed his cellmate.

'Do the guards know what happened?' I asked. He shot me a look of disgust. 'No,' he told me. 'I'm not a grass.' Surely it was obvious what had happened. There were only two of them in the cell and he hadn't slashed himself. 'He did it by mistake,' he scowled. 'So that's what you say if anyone asks you.'

I hadn't realised that the 'no grassing' rule applied so rigidly. I knew that it was against the rules to tell tales to the guards but not that it was such a necessity to lie to cover other people's tracks for them. Still, Wayne had enough on his plate without having extra time added to his sentence. He had obviously snapped under the pressure. He was placed in the medical unit for observation until further notice.

I was also shocked at how well his cellmate had taken being attacked with a razor blade. 'It's not the first time,' he told me. 'I've been shot twice, stabbed in the ankle, the leg, the thigh, the back, the side of the body, the back of the neck, the head, the nose, the arm . . .' He was like a walking catalogue of injuries. 'Then I've been hit in the arm with a pickaxe, bitten by a pit bull and beaten by cops with riot batons.' A few stitches were clearly a drop in the ocean to him.

Wayne was transferred to another prison. The guards knew what he had done but couldn't prove it. They were faced with a wall of silence – no one on the wing would tell them anything. The consensus among the other prisoners was that his cellmate had deserved to be slashed for not letting Wayne watch his programmes on TV. 'There's two people gotta live in there,' Bolty told me. 'He can't just watch what he wants all the time and expect his pad mate [cellmate] to take it.' No one seemed to see a slashing as anything out of the ordinary. 'We've all had it done to us at one point or another,' another inmate told me. 'I got done in the back with a craft knife – they snapped the blade off so that I couldn't get it out. I had to pull it out myself and get my bird to stitch it up.' I felt like a fish out of water. To me, being sliced open was a pretty big deal. To these people, it was part of life.

The events of that night reminded me of what a lawless environment I was living in. If another prisoner was to stab me, no one would know who did it or why. It would be hushed up. I was locked in a place where petty arguments ended in bloodshed and nobody cared – not even the person on the receiving end. I made a mental note to let my cellmate watch whatever he wanted on television. It had been easy to pass Wayne off as harmless and forget that he was in prison for stabbing someone. My cellmate had stabbed his ex-girlfriend 20 times. It was a reminder that I was never truly safe, no matter how much I got used to prison life.

CHAPTER 4

WILLY

There were some very dangerous people in prison. Some of them seemed to operate outside of any code of morality and were, to all intents and purposes, complete psychopaths. They were predators who preyed on the weak and took great pleasure in doing so. Among the very worst of them was a guy called Willy.

Like most people in prison, Willy had grown up on a rough council estate where the man who had the most respect was the one who could throw the best punch. He had aspired to be a hard man from an early age and he was frequently suspended from school for fighting. By the age of 14 he had stopped going altogether and chose to fill the time in other ways – mainly hanging around on street corners with his mates and smoking weed. He was also selling it, although most of what he sold wasn't actually weed. 'I used to shot [sell] them herbal tea,' he grinned. 'The funny thing was, they kept coming back for more and telling me how good it was!'

By the time he was 15, harder drugs had been added to the menu. Every Friday night he would take speed and acid and get into even more trouble. The fact that he was taking Class A drugs so regularly at such an early juncture in his life was a telltale sign of things to come. He was never one to stand on the sidelines and watch other people get off their faces. He had to be there in the thick of it, gurning his face off and taking things to the extreme.

On his 16th birthday an event took place that changed Willy's life for ever. He took his first E. Whereas he had got a buzz from the speed and the acid trips, this was something else. Sights and sounds appeared more vivid, women were tear-jerkingly beautiful and he felt as though he were deeply in love with anyone and everything and that they all loved him back. 'That was back when pills were real pills,' he told me. 'They cost a tenner a pill but they were worth every penny.'

It wasn't long before Willy was taking Es nearly every night of the week. I can't imagine this being particularly enjoyable – taking ecstasy two nights in a row is enough to leave you feeling like your brain has been placed in a washing machine. Still, excess typified his life. If he enjoyed something he would do it again and again regardless of the consequences. He would travel to raves up and down the country – some illegal and some legal, some in abandoned warehouses and some in vast areas of forest – a hundred per cent of the attendees being on ecstasy pills.

The next major buzz Willy discovered was to be found in joyriding. It was a favourite pastime of the youths on his estate and if they could do it then so could he. The best car thieves in the area were highly exalted and even had their own groupies, known as 'TWOC slags' (TWOC being an acronym for both *t*aking *w*ithout *o*wner's *c*onsent and slang for a stolen car). He wanted a piece of the limelight and was willing to risk life and limb to get it. Soon he was driving cars at speeds of up to 160mph while off his head on speed and ecstasy with no regard for his safety, let alone that of other road users. A police car in hot pursuit was seen as more of a bonus than a threat to him – to get a chase off a cop car was the ultimate accolade. Some nights he would deliberately throw bricks at patrolling officers and then zoom off at high speed, hoping they would give chase. 'Sometimes there were as many as ten different TWOCs left around the estate,' he told me. 'A couple of times they had to get the helicopters onto us!'

Not everyone was as chuffed by Willy's death-defying antics as he was. The situation on the estate had got so bad that the residents were beginning to take things into their own hands. Concerned about their children's safety, a number of vigilantes teamed up to try to cull the number of joy riders. They would attempt to run Willy and his friends over whenever they saw them and were always trying to fight with them. 'They got battered every time, though!' Willy almost seemed to revel in the fact that the creators of chaos had triumphed over those attempting to restore some sense of order to the place.

'We were unstoppable,' Willy gloated. 'Soon we were starting to make a healthy wage from it as well. We started off taking the CD players and the alloys and then started targeting cars people wanted for ringing. We could get £90 for a decent CD player and £150 for each set of alloys.' This was the turning point. Car crime was now starting to become a job as opposed to a hobby. 'Ringing' is the act of taking the registration and chassis numbers from a car that is ready for scrapping and attaching them to a stolen car in order to sell it on. More business-minded criminals in the area had heard of Willy's aptitude for TWOCing and recruited his services to obtain said vehicles. He was told to target specific models of car that were stolen to order along with high-performance sports cars, which could be found outside high-class hotels and leisure centres.

Willy was making at least £200 a night. Sometimes he would steal as many as five cars in a single session. At 17 he developed a sideline in ram raiding. He would smash through the front of a shop window in a TWOC and grab as much as he could carry before jumping back into the driver's seat and speeding off into the night. He wouldn't even pay for the petrol he had used – he would simply pump it in and then put his foot down firmly on the accelerator.

A few of Willy's mates at the time were doing house

burglaries and he decided to tag along. It was unfamiliar territory to him, as all his other crimes had involved motor vehicles, but he had grown accustomed to taking other people's property, so it was no big thing to him. He was branching out and diversifying. He would do around five houses a day and make in the region of £500 from each one, aiming for TVs, camcorders and Sega Megadrives, as these were the easiest items to sell on. All his burglaries took place during broad daylight as night burglary carried a harsher sentence. While the occupants of the houses were out at work he was rifling through their belongings, searching for anything of value he could sell.

One particularly successful graft was on the house of a prolific commercial burglar who lived close by. His house was crammed to the ceiling with thousands of pounds' worth of designer clothes stuffed into black bin bags. This guy must have been making a fortune – too bad he hadn't kept his stash better hidden. It put ideas into Willy's head, though. If this guy was making this much from burgling shops and businesses, maybe commercial burglaries could be an avenue worth exploring.

One of Willy's first grafts on commercial premises was as the result of a tip-off from an employee. One of his friends had suggested stealing the expensive welding equipment from his place of work and had managed to get his hands on the keys and alarm codes. This made things a whole lot easier. There was no need for breaking and entering – he could effectively just walk in and walk out with the gear. The job went even better than he expected and he managed to come away with a lot more than just the welding equipment. He ended up getting computers, photocopiers, fax machines and £1,800 in petty cash – the takings literally filled the garage of the fence who bought it all off him. The fence offered him two grand for the lot – one grand straightaway and one later when he had the money. This would have been fair if he had stuck to the agreement and paid the second instalment but after the first payment he mysteriously stopped answering his phone and was never in when Willy and his mates called round. He was trying to pull a fast one.

'It got to the point where we were outside his house with bats shouting at him and he still wouldn't come out!' This was the first time weapons had been mentioned. Although he had got into a few fistfights during his schooldays, most of Willy's crimes so far had been of a nonviolent nature. The problem with entering the world of the professional criminal was that, if somebody welshed on a deal, there was no way of making them pay up without using force, and lots of it. If he intended to maintain his reputation he would have to make an example of this guy.

'One day I saw him in town,' Willy told me, a big grin spreading across his face in anticipation of his tale of revenge. 'I was drunk and high on Es at the time, so I ran to my car, got a hammer and smashed him all over with it. I kicked him in the head so hard there was blood pissing all over the street.' He described his actions as if they were something that had happened in a computer game as opposed to something that could have left someone with permanent brain damage. To him it was a necessary part of the job – a part he was to grow very fond of.

To live his life in the manner to which he was rapidly growing accustomed, Willy needed as much money as he could get. He had a very addictive personality and was not only drinking heavily and taking drugs on a nightly basis but had also developed a serious gambling problem. He was easily spending in the region of a few thousand pounds a week, at least £500 of which went on slot machines. He even went as far as to get a nine-to-five job at one point in the hope that it would earn him a few extra quid, but all it did was confirm the fact that it was not the life for him. He was very underwhelmed with the pay – he was used to earning in excess of £100 an hour, not a measly £5.70.

'Laptopping was the way forward back then!' Yet another illicit source of funding for his multiple addictions. Laptopping means stealing laptops left in parked cars – nothing particularly clever or elaborate there. Still, the money was good. He would get eight or nine laptops a day at £500 each and, while he was at it, he would rip out the CD player as well. 'You could get a good £80 for a player with a multi-changer.' It didn't even seem to register with him that these were other people's belongings – he talked about them as if he were somehow entitled to them because they had been left unattended. 'The best place to find laptops was motorway service stations 'cause that's where all the businessmen stopped for their dinner. If you saw a suit or a briefcase in a car, it was most likely a businessman's. Some days we'd go to 30 or 40 different car parks – one day we went all the way to London doing every single service station along the way.'

The blatancy of Willy's actions was, in a strange way, what helped them to pass undetected. Passers-by would assume that surely no one would be brazen enough to break into a car park full of cars in the middle of the day, so they gave him the benefit of the doubt and continued on their way. He was now working 12-hour days and putting in some real graft. From 9am until 9pm he was out robbing and stealing, and slowly his income crept up to a good four grand a week. The good thing about laptopping was that, even if he got caught, the maximum sentence for theft from a motor vehicle was still relatively low; and, besides, he had a police scanner and would listen in and pre-empt the Old Bill's every move. 'And if anyone ever tried to play the hero we'd just jump in a car and drive at them!' This was incredible. Was it really worth killing someone for trying to stop him from stealing a laptop? 'It's what has to be done,' he replied. 'Some people I know are doing manslaughter sentences for it.

'It wasn't all running people over, though,' Willy added, attempting to lighten the mood a little. 'We had a laugh too.' This 'laugh' consisted of stealing his victims' mobile phones, ringing up their friends and families and taunting them. A favourite was to text their wives and tell them that they'd met another woman. He had a very sadistic sense of humour.

Another thing that Willy had found funny was racism. 'I'm not really that racist but every now and again we'd go Paki bashing – just for a laugh,' he told me. It somehow made it worse that he genuinely didn't seem to have anything against Asians and that he just seemed to find the idea of victimising someone because of the colour of their skin amusing. He went on to describe in great detail a brutal racial attack in which he beat up and robbed an Asian taxi driver on a drunken night out. 'I was so pissed up that I kept trying to hit him when he was on the floor and missed and hit the kerb. I ripped my knuckles clean open – we were both covered in blood. I thought I'd killed him.' Didn't he feel any guilt at all? 'Yeah,' he replied. 'When I was sober I always felt guilty but then I would go and do the same again the next week.' Clearly, any remorse he was ever capable of feeling was very short-lived. He was an exceptionally cruel individual.

The nature of Willy's crimes was getting more and more extreme. He had started out with drug taking and car crime – a nuisance to society but nothing particularly sinister. However, the deeper he got into the criminal underworld the darker his life became. He was now associating with some very dangerous people.

The key to being a good thief is networking. Most professional crooks have connections who can get rid of a wide range of different goods at the drop of a hat, and fences and ringers are a thief's best friend. Some of these people aren't to be messed with.

One such character was a guy called Tommy. Tommy's dad was a member of a well-known organised-crime group. Tommy had been trying to gain membership too but they had cut him short at the prospecting stage because he was smoking crack cocaine regularly and this was a big no-no. This had left him feeling pretty pissed off. To make matters worse, one of his good friends had been sleeping with his daughter. After a few days of brutal punishment beatings Tommy was lenient enough to let him leave with his life but the whole business had left him in a stinking mood. On the plus side, he had this new connection who was bringing in top-class cars for him to ring and strip down for parts. This guy was Willy. He liked Willy – he was reliable. It was for this reason that he decided to use him for a few other things as well.

'Whenever someone needed their legs breaking or their head stamping on he knew that I'd be up for it,' said Willy of their relationship. One of them needed people's heads kicking in, the other liked kicking people's heads in. It was a match made in heaven. 'He was a good source of work but he could be a bit crazy at times.' One such occasion was the time when Tommy had pistol-whipped him and put a gun to his head. Willy had made the mistake of going to visit his daughter with the guy who had been having the fling with her. Although it must have looked bad, they had genuinely gone round for a social call and nothing else.

Tommy wasn't having any of it. He had come home high on crack and in a foul temper to see two men in his house fraternising with his innocent little princess. He roared with rage and immediately began to gun-butt the two men into submission. 'Get on the floor!' he yelled. They dropped to their knees. He put the gun to Willy's temple. This was it – he could either make a run for it or end up with a bullet in his head. He darted towards the nearest open window and dived out, distracting Tommy just enough for his friend to do likewise. A lucky escape – who knows what might have happened if they had stayed there? They had a few minor cuts and bruises but other than that they were both OK.

'I won't lie – it was pretty terrifying!' he told me. 'The next day he tried to ring us up like it was all a joke. Obviously he knew that we were useful if anybody needed doing in and wanted to keep things cool with us. We just went along with him like, "Yeah yeah, Tommy . . . erm . . . good joke."'

Being affiliated with such characters meant that it was only a matter of time before a jail sentence reared its head. 'I can't remember what I went down for,' he told me, 'but when I got out the price of laptops had halved.' The laptops had been his main graft – what was he to do now? 'I'd heard a lot of people in jail talking about selling drugs and they seemed to be making a lot of money, so I thought, How hard can it be?' The answer was not hard at all, provided you have the necessary muscle to ward off those wishing to sell on your patch or tax your earnings.

Rather than start off as a street dealer, Willy decided to begin at the top. He immediately set about assembling a workforce who would put the drugs out for him so that all he had to do was drop them off ready for distribution and collect the takings at the end of the day. All of the street dealers were smackheads and he treated them 'like shit', paying them £75 for each 13-hour day they worked. This averaged out at around £5.77 an hour – hardly a decent wage considering the risk involved. The current minimum wage is £5.73 – they were getting four pence more than this. They were being exploited in the worst possible way.

Willy provided all his employees with a mobile phone so that the drug users could get in touch with them and told them that it needed to be on from 9am until 10pm every day or they would suffer the consequences. As many addicts would ring for crack or heroin as soon as they knew the lines were open, it was essential that they could get through dead on 9am, as this was the busiest part of the day. If anyone's phone was off at ten past nine they would get their legs and arms broken or have slabs of concrete smashed down on their heads. To maintain control and cement his status as a drug lord as opposed to a mere runner, Willy knew he needed to be ruthless. The only way to command respect was through fear.

The drugs were considerably less effort than the laptops had been, and brought in a lot more cash. As he was the main crack and heroin dealer in his area, anyone else who wanted to sell these drugs would have to either work for Willy or buy their drugs from him, or else they would be badly hurt. 'They'd get stabbed up or their bones shattered with hammers,' he casually informed me, revelling in his own sadism and lack of compassion.

It wasn't hard to tell when someone was trying to move in on his patch – it was noticeable straightaway by the dip in sales. He would question his customers, find out who they had been scoring off and then ring up the dealer, requesting large quantities of drugs from them. When he saw their car approaching he would ram it off the road and then jump out with a few of his friends armed with baseball bats and samurai swords. This was when they learned never to stray into his territory ever again. 'One guy we ran a Stanley knife from the top of his head to the bottom of his face and then stabbed him in both legs and took his drugs from him,' Willy grinned. 'This other time I heard that these two birds were selling in our area. We had a long debate over what to do about it – my mate was saying, "Nah, we can't do anything to them – they're women," but at the end of the day business is business so we went down and stabbed them up.'

Some of these dealers tried to fight back. Willy had been shot at on several occasions and a few of his friends had received bullet wounds. This was a risky business. There was little chance of ending up in a body bag through stealing laptops or doing a few burglaries, but the rewards here were far greater. The average heroin addict probably spends around £1,000 a week on smack, so a single customer could bring in a grand a week.

To gain customers in any business, legal or illegal, advertising is an essential tool. You need to let people know about the goods or services that are being provided. Willy couldn't openly advertise what he was doing but he did the next-best thing. He printed off his runners' phone numbers onto pieces of card, laminated them and posted them through the letterboxes of all the known crack and heroin addicts in the area. He also left them in phone boxes, as many smackheads had traded in their mobile phones for drugs and had to use payphones to call their dealers. Soon he had a good hundred regular customers.

Just as business was booming it was cut short by another jail sentence. 'I've done so many of them I can't remember what this one was for either!' he exclaimed. 'It was good in a way, though, because I could make more from selling drugs in jail than I did on the out.' This was true – I had witnessed dealers behind bars making a small fortune from heroin, weed, steroids and Subutex. There wasn't much demand for stimulants, as people didn't want to be kept up all night when they couldn't sleep during the day because their cellmates would be up. Drugs were smuggled into the prison in people's rectums, wrapped in clingfilm and covered in hand cream for ease of entry. They were also thrown over the walls, wrapped in a thick layer of bubble wrap to avoid their contents spilling out across the yard.

Willy was putting out heroin and Subutex – he didn't really bother with weed or steroids. He was also selling mobile phones. These are prohibited in British jails and can go for £200 to £300 per phone. Again, they are smuggled in internally and are used for anything from arranging drugs packages to be thrown over the wall to organising executions. This happened in the case of Nigel Ramsey of Burngreave, Sheffield, who was on the same wing as I was when he was accused of ordering the fatal shooting of a 16-year-old gang member, Tarek Chaiboub. If it hadn't been for a mobile phone sold to him by someone like Willy, his young victim might still be alive today.

The first rule of selling hard drugs is never to get high on your own supply. This has been the downfall of many a major dealer. If you are selling something day in and day out, there is always a temptation to sample your own wares. Heroin is not a recreational drug. There is no one who just has a few puffs on a smack pipe every weekend to unwind, although there are many addicts who have convinced themselves that this is the case. To try it is to fall victim to it – and some may say it was justice that the drug with which Willy had ruined so many other people's lives was to have such a negative impact upon his own.

'I was in this jail where I didn't know many people and I was bored. I decided to see what all the fuss was about.' Bad move. He would soon be spending £100 a week on smack, which is a lot of money bearing in mind that cash is worth five times more in jail due to the added effort of having people send it in for you. 'Heroin warps your mind. It makes you deny your addiction, even to yourself. My mates were coming in on visits and seeing that I was losing weight but I couldn't see it at the time. To me there was nothing wrong with me.' The drug was taking over – it was in control now. Anyone who tried to persuade him to stop was deluded and he was the only one thinking straight. The smack soothed his pain. It made him forget what a negative life he was leading and wrapped his brain up in cotton wool. While he was smoking heroin he was in bliss. The rest of the time he was shivering and shaking and desperately craving more.

Towards the end of his sentence, Willy began to realise that he had a serious addiction. He was taking smack every day and experiencing crippling physical withdrawal symptoms whenever he was forced to go without it. His friends and associates on the outside would not approve of this. His respect on the street would plummet – he had lowered himself to the level of the people he had slapped about for turning on their phones a few minutes late. Something had to be done, so he decided to go cold turkey. This was easier said than done. It was three weeks of insomnia, depression, constant sweating and itching, diarrhoea, cramps and fever. He barely slept a wink and the few times he did manage to drift off he had vivid nightmares and woke up in a cold sweat. However, at the end of it all, normality was finally restored. He was no longer a slave to his brown chemical master. He was a free man.

Willy was soon a free man in the literal sense as well. Despite having had postal orders sent in regularly by his various criminal associates, he was flat broke. He had spent all his money on drugs. His friends were not amused. 'Don't ever take that stuff again,' they told him. They also showed him a way he could earn his money back again. During his absence, a few of his mates had started growing their own weed and decided to let him in on the tricks of the trade. Weed was less risky than crack or heroin as it was a Class C drug, meaning that the maximum penalty for selling it was considerably lower. Maybe this was the way forward. After all, there were a lot more people who smoked weed than piped crack or heroin. Why not give it a try?

In order to grow weed you need money to buy the expensive lighting equipment that is required. This was a problem – although not for long, as there are always ways of upping your funds if you have no concern for those you hurt along the way. Rather than constantly commit lesser crimes that would bring in drabs of cash here and there, Willy decided that he would become involved in something far more serious that would earn him large amounts of money straight away. He had a friend who was involved in 'tie-ups' – tying people up and robbing them in their own homes – and wanted in on it. This would carry a hefty sentence if he got caught but could bring in tens of thousands of pounds a time. Tie-ups worked from tip-offs by those who knew people who kept large amounts of cash or jewellery in their houses. They would ring up and tell him how much was stashed away and he would give them a cut of the takings after the robbery. Sometimes these people had made their money through crime but a lot of the time they were perfectly innocent, law-abiding citizens who just happened to be quite wealthy. Tie-ups could be incredibly brutal and often involved torture as a means of extracting the location of the stash.

'The minute we got in the house we'd hit them with something just to let them know who was boss!' Willy was getting excited now. This was something he took great pleasure in. 'We were good to them, really. Other people I know would have ran in and shot them in the legs, just to put the fear in them.' It got worse. 'This one guy, we burned him with stun guns and hit him all over his body with hammers and he still wouldn't tell us where the money was. Some people are greedy – it's their own greed that causes them the pain, really.' Willy seemed to have no conscience whatsoever. 'We'd use all sorts on them – bolt cutters, bats, hammers . . . Anything that would get them to tell us where the stash was.'

As well as doing tie-ups, Willy had a few other grafts on the go. He would wait until pub employees were carrying the day's takings to the bank, punch them in the face and take their money. This also relied upon tip-offs, as he would need to know the exact time they would be setting off and what route they would be taking. In the absence of such tip-offs, he was to be found selling cocaine at the local pub. He would buy an ounce for £550 and sell it at £40 a gram, although what he passed off as a gram was actually only four-fifths of a gram. He was making a good four grand a week from this but he was also beginning to snort a lot of coke. A good percentage of his profit went straight up his nose.

Soon, all his hard work had paid off and Willy had earned enough to invest in his own growing equipment. He decided to set up a partnership with one of his mates who had grown his own weed before. Their first crop yielded 56 plants, earning an impressive £21,000 between the two of them. All of the plants were being grown in his mate's spare bedroom – from the outside it looked innocuous but inside it could have easily passed for a garden centre.

Things were back on track. All the cash that had gone on smack was now fully recouped, plus more. All that was needed now was for Willy to take his rightful place as the local neighbourhood drug lord. Sure he was making enough from weed and coke but why stop there? There were plenty of crackheads and smackheads itching for a fix and it was just a case of supply and demand. With the cash he had gained from all of his other endeavours he bought himself a mountain of brown and white and set about recruiting some new runners to peddle his wares.

In order to keep his house drug-free in case the police came knocking, Willy would bury his supplies in a nearby field in sealed plastic beakers to prevent them from getting moist. This proved problematic because, the minute a smackhead got a whiff of where the drugs were kept, they would try to dig them up and steal them. 'Some of them were relentless,' he said. 'We burned them with kettles and all sorts and they still kept coming back looking for where I'd buried them the next day.'

What with the epidemic of drug addicts that Willy had created, his area was now rife with burglary, but in typical fashion he seemed fairly blasé about the whole affair. If it wasn't the house of someone he knew, he didn't care – it was a case of out of sight, out of mind. 'Mind you, there was this one time when this guy managed to rack up £800 of debt with us.' I knew exactly where his story was going. 'And he went out robbing to try to get the money. He made the mistake of trying to rob my brother's bird's house. I gave him a right good hiding when I caught him – I must have stabbed him over 20 times and caved his face in with a house brick. By the end of it, he looked like the elephant man.' To say that violence dominated his life was an understatement. It seemed to be his answer to everything.

There is an obvious flaw in an ex-heroin addict's decision to sell heroin – namely, temptation. The sight of large bags of skag sitting on a table in front of even the most dedicated of former junkies would be enough to make them relapse. Willy was to lapse in and out of addiction. He would get hooked, go cold turkey and then become addicted again when the temptation got too much to bear. Curiosity had also caused him to try the other main substance he was selling – crack. Although there are fewer physical symptoms from withdrawing from crack than heroin, it is still highly addictive. It wasn't long before he was smoking up to five grand's worth a week.

Would it not have been a lot easier to have spent less on drugs so there would have been no need to do so much crime to afford them? It would have kept him out of jail, for one thing. 'Jail is a graft in itself,' Willy explained. 'There are enough ways to get paid in here and I don't just mean the drugs and the phones. There's people need things done that only a guy like me can do.' Clearly, incarceration was no real obstacle for him in his quest for money and drugs. 'Like this fella finds out this guy's a nonce and he pays me and my mate an eight-mil each to do him in. I smashed a coffee jar and rammed the glass into his face and my mate has this TV aerial he's sharpened up and sticks it straight in him.' Brutal stuff, although quite a mundane occurrence for him, judging by the way he told it.

Although he did have a fondness for stabbing, slashing, beating and bludgeoning, Willy wasn't always so hands-on in his approach. In order to avoid getting extra days added to his sentence or a lengthy spell in the segregation unit he would often delegate these tasks to someone lower in the prison hierarchy. 'I still got a share of the profit and all I had to do was organise it,' he told me. 'Then if anything went wrong it wouldn't come back on me. There was this guy who nearly got killed by mistake a few years back. He taxed a phone off this Yardie so the guy paid me to have someone slash him up. The geezer I got to do it went to slash him across the neck and the shiv got stuck and he couldn't get it out. He was there tugging on it for a good few minutes.' A shiv is a homemade prison weapon, usually consisting of a set of blades from a shaving razor melted into a toothbrush handle. Slashing someone across the neck with such an implement could have easily severed their jugular vein and killed them. If he carried on like this, Willy would soon be heading towards a murder charge.

'What do you think made you like this?' I asked, taken aback by the things I had heard. He shrugged his shoulders. 'I had a stable upbringing but my mum and dad were struggling a bit.' I had half expected some horrific event hidden in his past to have caused him to live his life like this. He had been poor but had suffered no real hardship. 'I guess I never had expensive trainers or fashionable clothes and I wanted the nice things in life,' he went on. So it was basically a question of need: he knew that there were certain things he would never have unless he stole them. But the extent to which he was willing to go to get these things was inexcusable, as was the fact that he seemed to derive a perverse pleasure from everything bad he'd done to people. 'Don't you ever feel guilty?' I asked. 'Sometimes,' he replied, 'but it soon goes away.'

The strangest thing about Willy was that in his day-to-day life he was basically very normal. He seemed to be able to switch from a rational, functional human being to a rabid animal when there was an advantage to be gained from doing so. It was as though he had two separate personalities he could call on at will – one for when he was doing crime and one for the rest of his life. He was fairly diplomatic and had sorted out a few disputes involving other factions within the prison. You might have thought he would be encouraging them to tear chunks out of each other but this was not the case. He was a very contradictory and complex character.

'What are you going to do when you get out then?' I asked him, already half knowing the answer. A toothy grin spread across his face. 'Oh, lots of things,' he told me. 'You'll probably see me on the news in a few months' time for doing something particularly horrific to someone.' This was what perplexed me. He was clearly a sane person and he was capable of being moralistic – I had seen him act like this on many occasions on the wing. He just seemed to prefer being immoral. He found it amusing. Maybe being a criminal was his true calling in life. Jail was definitely the best place for him as far as the rest of society was concerned.

For someone who had supposedly kicked his heroin addiction, not a day went by in prison when Willy wasn't on some kind of drugs. Most of the time it was Subutex, although he would still take heroin whenever he could get his hands on it, flooding the wing with it on several occasions. He had it thrown over the walls, brought back by those who were permitted town visits and even surreptitiously passed across during visits with his friends and relatives. 'Go on, have a boot with us!' he would implore me whenever I walked past his cell. A 'boot' is slang for a heroin pipe. He would tell me that he now only took smack in prison to pass the time. It was just something to do and he would quit as soon as he got out.

These were all excuses. To me the sight of a former heroin addict smoking heroin again meant only one thing: that he was back on it. Drugs would always dominate his life. They would remain his main motivation for years to come, and as long as he still enjoyed getting high he would do anything and everything to ensure that he could buy more of them. He was a one-man crime wave driven by a highly excessive lifestyle. Of all the people I met in jail I would say he was the most likely to reoffend. Crime was his life. Without it he would have nothing.

CHAPTER 5
MAHIR

While some prisoners had lived stable if somewhat impoverished lives during their early years, there were inmates who had led turbulent and unpredictable existences from day one. Although there is no excuse for living a life of crime, it was easy to see why they had chosen to go down this path. Some had grown up in Third World conditions. Quite literally.

Mahir was born in Somalia during a bloody civil war. He had seen his cousin shot and killed inches from his face and had held an AK-47 at just six years old. It was a place where hatred was rife and you could be brutally murdered just for being from a different tribe. Life was cheap and the landscape was ravaged by famine and disease. Somalia was basically in a state of anarchy and anyone who could get away did so. Fearing for their safety, his family had scraped together enough money to flee to England and start a new life. Seven-year-old

Mahir had packed his bags and trailed behind his mother to Mogadishu Airport. It was time to leave the war zone behind.

'We had to stop off in Moscow first,' Mahir explained. 'It was snowing there – I'd never seen snow and never seen white people before!' He laughed as he told me this. For all the trials and tribulations he had experienced he still seemed to me far less corrupted than his fellow inmates. He was very warm and friendly and had a kindly demeanour to him. He seemed to genuinely enjoy telling me about his life and relished the opportunity to share his story. 'We stayed in Russia for two days and then flew over to Manchester and settled in Moss Side.' Out of one war zone and into another, although it was still a great improvement on Somalia.

Britain was certainly different from anything he had experienced before. The girls were cheeky, even the Somalian ones! They answered back and told you exactly what they thought of you if you stepped out of line. Still, the people were friendlier and less hostile and day-to-day life was fairly relaxed. He was living on a council estate with nine people crammed into a three-bedroom house, but to him it wasn't too bad. Things could have been a lot worse. He knew plenty of people who hadn't made it this far.

Mahir learnt English in no time at all and did consistently well at school. He was bright and picked things up easily. He got along well with his fellow pupils and found it easy to adapt to the British way of life. The only thing that set him aside from his peers was his attitude to death. To him it was just part of life and nothing to be afraid of. His classmates would think it was a big thing when someone got shot or killed on the estate, whereas as far as he was concerned it was nothing. In his home country, hundreds of people had died all around him every day. Guns and knives were just objects. They made no more impact in his mind than a spoon or a piece of paper.

Being a member of a strict Muslim family could be somewhat stifling. Mahir was religious but did not adhere strictly to the principles of Islam. It was difficult for his parents to keep a watchful eye on him as he had so many brothers and sisters for them to look after, and it wasn't long before he began to rebel. 'I started hanging out on street corners and my friends became as much of a family as my actual family was,' he told me. At 13, he began spending more and more time round at an older friend's house smoking weed. This friend controlled the majority of the drugs trade in Moss Side and had ties to the Gooch gang, who were responsible for a number of high-profile murders in the area. If his parents had known the company he was keeping they would have been mortified.

The Gooch gang, taking its name from nearby Gooch Close, was one of several that operated in Moss Side. Local youths would stake a claim to certain roads and streets as their patch and were averse to anyone entering them unannounced. There was also tension between different racial groups within the region. Whereas most people tended to get along, there were those in the Afro-Caribbean community who did not like Somalians. People tend to assume that black people are one large harmonious, homogeneous group, but this is simply not the case. During my time in prison I witnessed prejudice from Jamaican inmates towards Africans, Asians and even those from nearby Trinidad and Tobago, who were referred to as 'monkey eaters'. Mahir would soon find out the hard way that there were certain areas where he simply wasn't welcome.

'People think they own certain streets in Moss Side,' he smiled, clearly smart enough to know how ridiculous this was but at the same time accepting that it was just the way things were. 'These two boys tried to tell me I shouldn't be on their patch 'cause I was Somalian and they were Jamaican. They pulled blades out on me but I wasn't scared. I'd had my life threatened before on more than one occasion, so I chose to stand my ground.' This was either very brave or very stupid – possibly the latter, as he was consequently stabbed in the arm and sliced across the stomach. However, it was events like this that helped to create his reputation as a fearless street warrior. This was something that older gangsters within the area would soon pick up on and use to their advantage.

Rather than avoiding areas in which there was likely to be conflict, 14-year-old Mahir moved out of his parents' house and went to live with his uncle on Claremont Road. This was the road separating the territories of the two main gangs in the area – Gooch and Doddington.

While a lot of his friends were in the Gooch, he had to walk through Doddington turf to get to places he needed to go. Instead of skirting around this area, he would plough straight through the middle. Despite his young age, his attitude was beginning to impress senior figures within the Gooch.

As well as being fearless, Mahir was known for being loyal, trustworthy and generally a good kid. Whereas many on his estate were sly and scheming, he had managed to keep his integrity intact. It was for this reason that major gangland figures had (allegedly) chosen him to deliver drug packages for them. They knew that he wouldn't steal any of the drugs and take them himself, and they were confident that he wouldn't back down if someone tried to rob him. 'If someone stuck a gun in my face I'd stick one back in theirs,' he stated. 'If you give in, they will do it every day.'

And so during the day he was working hard for his GCSEs and in the evening he was (allegedly) transporting crack and heroin across the slums of south Manchester. He excelled in both domains. He got eight A–Cs in his exams and managed to develop a formidable rep on the streets. He preferred the street life to school but kept going to please his parents, as he didn't want to let them down. They had worked hard to bring him to this country and the least he could do was to try to make them proud.

To see a son kitted out in the latest clothes and trainers without any legitimate source of income would be an immediate source of suspicion for even the most

trusting of parents. To cover his tracks, Mahir got a job
as soon as he was old enough. He worked part-time at
TK Maxx in Salford and told his parents that this was
where the money was coming from. Salford is a rough,
predominantly white, working-class city just west of
Manchester. The only time he had ventured into these
parts before was to fight with the local racists, who were
giving one of his friends there some trouble. He worked
there under a year and during this time the shop was
subject to two separate gunpoint robberies, most
probably from the locals, as this was something the city
was renowned for.

Time went by and Mahir quit his job. He was
heading to university in a few months and didn't feel
that working in a clothes shop was of any benefit to
him. Crime was the only job he needed for the time
being. His time at the shop had given him some food
for thought, though. The robbers had managed to get
away with large sums of money both times they had
struck. They had made a fair little earner from what
had been only a few hours' work per robbery. An idea
began to form in the back of his mind. The Salford
branch of TK Maxx was about to be robbed for a third
time. 'I knew where the safe was and I knew which
manager was on when and what they were like,' he
told me. 'If I was to have done the place over, it would
have been easy.' A cheeky grin spread across his face
from one side to the other.

Some time later Mahir was walking through
Manchester city centre carrying a plastic carrier bag

containing £5,000, covered by a layer of clothes from TK Maxx (more likely than not, from the Salford branch). He had done nothing to arouse suspicion and saw no way in which the police could have caught onto him. Unfortunately for him he had failed to allow for being on the receiving end of a random stop-and-search. It landed him in a whole heap of trouble. The serial numbers on the bank notes matched those of money that had been taken during an armed robbery in Salford. Of course, he knew nothing about this. He had merely been asked to deliver the bag by a third party.

It turned out that four masked figures, armed with guns and baseball bats, had smashed through the front window of TK Maxx and demanded that the manager open the safe. One of them had been roughly the same height and build as Mahir. Two of these men had been apprehended – they had removed their masks too soon in the car park and had been caught on CCTV in their getaway car. They were both from Moss Side. They would eventually get three years each but refused to reveal the identity of the other two robbers. Thirty thousand pounds had been taken from the safe, along with £15,000 worth of jewellery and money from the tills. Mahir had known nothing about any of this. All he had known was that money needed delivering and that he would be paid for acting as the courier. At least, that's what his solicitor had said in court.

'For the serious charge of conspiracy to commit armed robbery we find you not guilty!' This was a result. 'For the lesser charge of handling stolen property we find you guilty. However, seeing that you are set to make a new start at university this September, we have thought it best not to issue you with a custodial sentence.' This was even better – he'd been let off the hook. 'Therefore, I sentence you to 300 hours of community service.' He could do that standing on his head. It beat prison any day.

All the evidence pointed towards the fact that Mahir had planned the robbery and got away with it. The fact that he had worked in the branch of TK Maxx that had been robbed had strongly implicated him. But without proof what could they do? It had been a close call. He could have done a fair whack behind bars. Needless to say, he was very relieved. 'The judge had given me a chance, so I thought let's do what he says and make a fresh start,' he told me. 'My mum and dad weren't best pleased and I didn't want to be the black sheep of the family for ever!'

And so that September he started his pharmacy degree at Bradford University. Although academically gifted, he wasn't a big fan of education. It was more something he did to keep his parents happy. They would prefer him to be a chemist or a pharmacist rather than a drug dealer or armed robber. Choosing to give student halls the body swerve, he decided to move in with his sister in nearby Leeds. She lived in Chapeltown (or 'Chappy') – the area where Straps had been selling grenades and sub-machine-guns. Still, at least it was an improvement on his previous surroundings. 'Chappy was rough but it was a lot more relaxed than Moss Side – although that wasn't necessarily what I wanted!' Mahir smiled at the absurdity of this statement. 'I had got used to life in the ghetto. Still, you could walk anywhere and didn't get people confronting you, so it was good in that way.'

The time at university went without a hitch. He got a 2.1 in his final exams and managed to stay out of trouble. He had been doing some part-time work as a security guard and was even slowly paying off his student loan. The problem in his family now lay elsewhere. His dad had lent an Asian shopkeeper a large amount of money and he was paying it back incredibly slowly, leaving his dad constantly short of funds. This incensed Mahir. The guy owned an expensive jewellery shop, so he clearly had enough money to pay it all back straightaway. Why should his dad suffer for trying to help him out? Something had to be done.

'I couldn't have him taking the piss like that!' he told me. 'My dad had worked hard for that money – he had always made an honest wage and it wasn't fair that this was being done to him.' There was truth in what he was saying but what he did next was nevertheless over the top. He masked up, ran into the jeweller's shop with a gun and helped himself to £50,000 worth of stock. In doing so, he made the fatal mistake of ripping one of his gloves and cutting his finger on a piece of broken glass.

Mahir's dad didn't want anything to do with the stolen jewellery. As he had stolen it for altruistic reasons and not for personal gain, Mahir decided to send it across to his family in Somalia instead. They were still living in Third World conditions and could not afford to turn down a prize like this, regardless of where it had come from. I had to admire him for not just keeping it all for himself. He had risked his freedom and hadn't gained a penny from it.

Bam! Mahir's sister's door came off its hinges. It was the police. 'We are arresting you on suspicion of armed robbery . . .' They had found a single drop of blood at the scene of the crime and had all the evidence they needed to convict him. 'You do not have to say anything but it may harm your defence if you do not mention, when questioned, something which you later rely on in court. Anything you do say may be given in evidence.' That was him put away for the next few years. Still, at least he hadn't sat back and let his family be taken for fools. He had been raised in a place where, if you didn't stick up for yourself, you ended up dead. He had done what he had to do.

Four years. That was his degree down the drain. Jail wasn't anything scary, though – it was a lot safer than living in Moss Side and there were plenty of ways to earn money. 'There were always people wanting smack,' he told me, a mischievous glint in his eyes. It wasn't hard to work out who was the one supplying it. 'Where there's demand there is also supply.'

Prison was an eye opener for Mahir in that it reminded him of just how much money could be made from selling drugs. His chances of getting a decent job were now quite slim, what with his having a criminal record for armed robbery. There was only one thing left for him to do, and that was to set up shop. Chapeltown was an open market for drugs – people came from as far afield as York and Harrogate just to get crack, and there was no shortage of addicts there waiting on a fix. Anyone who was white in the hardcore black estates had most probably come to score.

Mahir didn't want to go back to jail any time soon, so things would have to be done very carefully this time round. He couldn't have customers ringing his phone directly, because, if the police seized it and found records of hundreds of calls from phone boxes, it would look highly suspicious. All his calls were filtered through three different workers before they reached him and he had a friend delivering the drugs on his behalf, so he rarely met any of his clients face to face. All this was to no avail. It took only one wrong move and a bit of bad luck to land him firmly in the shit again.

One of the occasions when drugs had to be handed over personally was when he was selling large quantities to another drug dealer. Rather than deliver the full amount straightaway, Mahir would provide them with a sample to test on their customers and see if they liked it. He would usually go straight to the agreed meeting place without taking any detours along the way. This time it was his birthday – he was in high spirits and felt there was no need to rush. Despite being a practising Muslim, he had decided to get drunk to celebrate the occasion and had stopped off at the local off-licence. He bought a bottle of Jack Daniel's and a litre of Coke and then got chatting to some girls outside the shop. Here he was to have another stroke of misfortune.

'Ali Maalim, I am arresting you on suspicion of supplying Class A drugs . . .' Eh? What was this? He had never heard of Ali Maalim in his life. And how had the police known he had drugs on him? Then it dawned on him – it was a case of mistaken identity. As the cuffs closed tightly around his wrists and he was shepherded into the back of squad car, he began to protest his innocence loudly. He had been chatting trying to secure some female company for the night's festivities. 'I'm telling you, you've got the wrong guy!' Yeah, yeah. They'd heard it a million times before. The problem was that, although he was telling the truth, he had a wrap of heroin and several rocks of crack cocaine in his pocket. He was done for.

'I'm not the luckiest of people!' Mahir laughed. 'The worst thing is they had no evidence that I was selling it, just that I had it on me. I thought, There's no way they can have me for anything other than possession. So I decided to take it to trial. The problem was, they'd drug-tested me at the police station and I'd come up negative for crack and smack. I tried telling them I wanted to take some for the first time to celebrate my birthday but they weren't having it. I reckon if I was white and middle-class like you, I would have got off with it.' This was rich, coming from a guy who had effectively got community service for an armed robbery.

'How long did you get altogether, then?' I asked.

'Five years,' he replied. This was steep for a first drugs offence, I had to admit. 'And are you going to go back to it when you get out?' I followed up, curious to see if he had learned his lesson. 'Nah, it's not worth it,' he told me. 'I've done a plumbing course in here and I really want to get into that. You can make good money from it.'

So, in a way, the training he had received in jail had helped to rehabilitate him and had aided him in establishing a source of income other than crime. Of course, if he had stuck to his pharmacy degree in the first place he would have had his career path all mapped out for him, but temptation had got the better of him.

Mahir was not a bad person – he had just kept some bad company and made some bad choices. He came across as kind and gentle in his everyday life but strongly desensitised to the serious nature of the crimes he had committed. He was protective of the weaker inmates on the wing and seemed to me to be one of the few people in the jail with a strong sense of morality intact, even if it was a somewhat misguided one. I think in a way, like Bolty, he had needed a long sentence to give him time to reflect upon his life. Hopefully, when he got out, things would be different.

'See, I came from a place where you had to fight to survive,' he concluded. 'Even when I was in a peaceful place, I still had the fight in me. I had still seen certain things and felt certain emotions that wouldn't go away, even though I was young at the time.' I guess, clichéd as it was, you could take Mahir out of Somalia but you could never take Somalia out of Mahir. Or at least it would take time and a great deal of soul searching for him to do so. I wished him all the best – he was one of the few people I had met inside who had the potential for change.

CHAPTER 6
OLD MAN STEVE

Whereas Mahir had been born into acute poverty and his crimes were fuelled by his sense of youthful rebellion, another guy on the wing was the polar opposite. He was born into an affluent Jewish family and grew up distinctly middle-class. He had managed to live a crime-free life until he was in his early forties, when he was convicted of supplying crack and heroin to an undercover officer. He'd been living in relative comfort and had no need to be selling drugs, so it did prompt the question: what had driven him to this? Things are not always as simple as they seem.

Old Man Steve was a frail, elderly-looking man in his late fifties. It was hard to imagine he had done anything illegal in his life. He was constantly smiling and reminded me somewhat of the granddad from the Werther's Originals advert. He had been raised in the distinctly average West Yorkshire village of Queensbury and was well educated, having achieved a first in engineering at Bradford University. After completing his degree, he went on to manage a large company in Bingley, with 250 employees under him. Things started to go downhill when he found out his wife was having an affair. He'd seen her coming out of another man's house laughing and giggling and had immediately clocked what was going on. On being confronted, she had confessed everything. It had been going on for quite some time.

'I'd never hit a woman but let's put it this way – *he* moved out of the village pretty damn quickly!' he told me, his top lip curling into a half-snarl as he spoke. Steve's usually cheerful demeanour had quickly soured and this was obviously still a sore point for him. 'That's when my head went and I started drinking. I couldn't believe she'd done it to me. What a bastard. I would never, ever sleep with another man's wife.' At this point, he was getting visibly upset, so I hurried the conversation along to the matter in hand. 'So when did you first start selling the drugs?

'Well . . .' he began. It turned out that Steve had been a dab hand at rugby back in the day. He had played at a semi-professional level and then, when he was too old for that, just for fun. One day, after the match, the post-game conversation had drifted onto the topic of clothing. 'I know this guy who can get really cheap designer gear – not knock-offs, the real thing.' Steve's ears pricked up. 'How much are we talking?' he asked. 'Like three or four quid for stuff that would cost you

£20 in the shops.' Steve wasn't particularly hung up on designer clothing but could never resist a bargain. 'Where can I get hold of this bloke, then?' he enquired.

It turned out that 'this bloke' was a ram raider – he was selling all manner of stolen merchandise, from clothes to electrical goods. 'I still wasn't thinking straight,' Steve told me. 'My head was all over the place and I was on the bottle all the time. I'm not going to say anything that could incriminate me, but if I had wanted to I could have made a lot of money selling things on. The guy was selling 400 top-notch designer jumpers for £1,500 – I could have sold them for four grand in ten minutes flat, literally.' This was a profit of £250 per minute.

The ram raider was a heroin addict and he was stealing to feed his habit. 'He was always broke even though he was earning a grand-odd a week,' Steve said. 'It made me wonder how much he was actually spending on the stuff and gave me a few ideas.' It would be cheaper to pay him in drugs at a time when he was craving them rather than handing over the full amount of money. Steve had decided to become a drug dealer. The ram raider had put him onto a few of his friends who took smack and crack, and things had snowballed from there.

'I was buying an ounce for £120 and selling 0.2s [bags containing 0.2 grams] for £20 at first.' Humble beginnings. 'I used to do charity work with West Indians in Bradford and I had a few contacts there who were smoking crack as well, so I started selling to them.' It was ironic that the people he had been helping were now coming to him for drugs. He was slowly building up his clientele and moving gradually up the ladder from small-time accidental dealer to major drug peddler.

'I was putting out good stuff and it wasn't long before word got round.' By now he had quit his nine-to-five – there was no need for it. He was making two grand a day – enough to afford him expensive holidays in Jamaica and the Bahamas. He had always been a fan of West Indian music and now he had enough money to experience it first hand. The problem was that, now that he had flooded Queensbury with heroin, the burglary rate had shot right up. It was no longer safe to leave his house unattended while he jetted off across the world. After one of his exotic vacations, he came back to find his door had been kicked in and his things had been taken.

'The cheeky bastards!' Steve exclaimed. 'You see, not everyone who takes smack is like that. A lot of my customers held down nine-to-fives and worked for their drug money. But then you get the bad type of addict as well.' But hadn't the fact that he was selling stolen property created a market for this type of burglary? 'Yeah, but if I had been doing that, which I'm not saying I had, it would have been burglaries on shops – not people's houses.'

Steve was not best pleased that his house had been broken into and quizzed his customers to see if they knew anything about it. After a bit of detective work, he managed to get hold of the names and addresses of the culprits. 'I can't tell you what I did to them,' he grinned. 'But they won't be robbing my house again in a hurry.' The word on the wing was that he had taken them to Ilkley Moor, placed them in an oil drum full of water, suspended it above a fire and boiled them for a good few minutes. When they had been suitably scalded he had taken them out, stripped them of their clothes and sent them naked onto the moor to walk home.

'I hate thieves!' He had told me this over and over again. 'I've sold drugs but people have a choice whether they buy them or not. You don't have a choice whether you get your house burgled.' But it was drugs that had led to these burglaries, because of people stealing to fund their habits. 'People have free will,' said Steve. 'You can't blame a substance because you decide to steal someone's belongings. It's your own fault. I think all drugs should be legalised – then they wouldn't cost as much and there would be no need for people to steal. In the 1800s people were smoking opium legally and we never had any of this going on.'

Steve continued putting drugs out for a good few years until his first arrest. He was caught with large amounts of crack and heroin and received a two-year sentence. Not too bad, considering the amount of money he must have made altogether. His first time in jail was a particularly bad experience. He landed in a notoriously brutal jail in the East Midlands known as 'Bed Leg City' on account of the inmates' tendency to beat each other over the head with its heavy wooden bed legs. The staff were even worse than the prisoners. One time he was called into the office on suspicion of having drugs passed over on a visit. He was severely beaten and hidden away in the segregation unit until his injuries had healed before being allowed back on the main wing. 'It was a horrible place,' he told me. 'Barbaric!'

When he came out of jail, Steve found it difficult to find work even with his top-level degree. When he did finally gain employment at an engineering company it ended up going bust and he lost his job. There wasn't much on offer for someone with a criminal record for selling Class A drugs and he needed an income to survive. There was only one thing for it – do what he had done before, but try very hard not to get caught this time. 'This time there were three of us,' he told me. 'There was one guy on foot and me and this other guy in a car. We always took a bird with us so we could hide drugs up her.' He meant secreting the drugs in her vagina. She was being used as a drugs mule.

'We did Wibsey, Wyke and Low Moor in Bradford as well as Queensbury and parts of Cleckheaton and Brighouse.' None of these areas were known for being particularly rough – they were all fairly average. 'Then we had Jimmy walking it on the Allerton estate.' This is a large sprawling council estate known for crime and unemployment – more the type of area you would associate with widespread drug abuse. It definitely isn't the type of place you'd want to walk around all day on your own. 'He was making £1,500 a day just from the one estate. We were making £2,000 from all of our rounds put together.' The total takings were split among the three of them, so he made around £1,100 a day – more than some people earn in a month.

It is difficult to sell hard drugs like crack and heroin and stay safe while doing so. Danger is normally just around the corner. In Yorkshire, this danger usually came in the form of a shadowy figure known as the Taxman. He had acquired this name through his habit of robbing drug dealers and was something of a living legend. It seemed that nearly every dealer from Leeds or Bradford had encountered him at one point or another and a few of them had the scars to prove it. 'He was a complete and utter psychopath – he'd smoked far too much crack!' Steve could talk – he was probably the one who had sold it to him in the first place. 'I was dropping some brown off for this girl and he was there as well. They were meant to be going halves on it but he said she wasn't getting any unless she slept with him first. She said no and he pulled a gun out and started braying [hitting] her with it.' Steve wasn't one to sit back and watch someone beat up a girl – he had strong traditional values and immediately stepped in to try to calm things down. 'That's when he started letting shots off all over the place,' he said. 'He put the gun to my head, so I gave him a few rocks and said, "Here – if you want it that badly then have this as well." That seemed to pacify him.'

Steve was lucky to have come out of this situation alive, but the Taxman wasn't his only concern. With a drug-dealing operation of this magnitude it was only a matter of time before it all came crashing down. And that's exactly what it did. One day he left his house to find his driveway completely surrounded by police cars. This must have been a shock for his neighbour, who was a police officer and had been totally oblivious of what had been going on right under his nose. 'We are arresting you under suspicion of supplying Class A drugs.' He had crack and heroin on him and had been caught bang to rights. That was another few years of his life down the pan.

It was during this period that Steve had decided he no longer wanted to be a drug dealer. It wasn't worth spending half of his life in jail for any amount of money. You can't put a price on the years of your life, especially when you have a son. Children grow up so quickly and to miss out on the formative years of their lives can be devastating. So Steve decided to put it all behind him and start afresh – it had all been the result of what was basically a mental breakdown after his wife's affair. He had been reckless and irresponsible and it was time to grow up. After all, he was old enough to know better.

If only it was that easy. Jimmy had other ideas and the minute Steve was out he rang him up, asking to meet with him. Steve was apprehensive. 'I'm not going back to what we did before,' he told him bluntly. 'Just meet me and then we can discuss it,' Jimmy persuaded him. They met up at a hotel in Bradford city centre and Jimmy immediately tried to coax him back into selling drugs. 'It'll be just like before – we'll make a packet!' he said. But, try as he might, it was never going to happen. If only the Drug Squad had known this before they had come bursting through the door. 'Where are the drugs?' they bellowed. It wasn't exactly rocket science – they were in the tightly bound packages spread across the room in plain view. There was nothing to link Steve to the drugs other than the fact that he had been in the same room as they were. Jimmy's fingerprints were all over them. However, the concept of being innocent until proven guilty truly applies only to those with no previous convictions. Due to 'previous bad character', Steve was deemed to have had a part in preparing the drugs for sale and was sentenced to another five years in jail.

'If my mum was alive she would never have let it get that far!' he told me, somewhat regretfully. 'I was very stupid and I was going through a bad patch.' It seemed to me that his risk-taking behaviour had served as something of a distraction from the pain that he was feeling after the break-up of his marriage. People often take part in extreme and dangerous activities when they are severely depressed as a way of coping with their hurt.

Steve grew to be one of my good friends during my time inside, and you couldn't really have asked for a nicer bloke (apart from the burglar-boiling incident, which did sound quite disturbing). He admitted that what he had done was wrong, although he still had some funny ideas about the nature of drugs offences and thought that, compared to people who were committing burglaries, armed robberies and the likes, what he had done had been fairly minor. I guess whether you agree with this or not boils down to your personal opinions on drugs. I told him that I thought that crack and heroin had devastated communities. He remained adamant that this was down to the personal choices made by the users and that the substances themselves were not to blame. 'Heroin can even keep you healthy,' he told me. 'It stops you from getting colds. It was originally marketed as a cold medicine by a company in Germany.' This was a single benefit in a sea of negatives.

Steve was stubborn, but at the same time I felt he had learned from his mistakes. Now he was more likely to be mugged by a crackhead than sell them 0.2s. His drug-dealing days were long gone. It was time for him to live his life within the light as opposed to the shadowy world of the grafter. He had officially retired.

CHAPTER 7
BIRDMAN

Steve wasn't the only unlikely-looking criminal in the prison. There was another equally intriguing grey-haired old man who stood out like a sore thumb. He had no tattoos, his head was unshaven and he didn't look particularly threatening or aggressive. In fact, he walked around the wing in his dressing gown. Every time I saw him on the wing, I puzzled over what he might have done to land himself behind bars.

Inmates in most British jails have the choice of either working or doing an educational course to pass the time. The jobs usually involve cleaning the prison – I couldn't think of anything worse than spending my sentence scrubbing floors and picking up litter, so I opted for a computer course instead. I thought I might as well get another qualification and spend my time inside constructively. Besides, it was a good opportunity to meet inmates from the other wings and see what crimes they had done.

There were four other prisoners on the course: a neo-Nazi who was learning to program HTML so he could make a website dedicated to Hitler; an ageing Mancunian gangster; an Asian heroin dealer from Bradford; and the curious grey-haired old man. 'What are you in for?' I asked the Nazi. 'Wounding with intent and witness intimidation,' he told me. 'I broke some guy's legs with a bat.' Probably not someone white, at a guess. 'I'm in for selling gear,' chimed in the heroin dealer. The Mancunian gangster stayed quiet. 'What about you?' I asked the grey-haired man. 'Armed robbery,' he replied.

I hadn't expected him to have done anything that serious. I had assumed that he was in for fraud or tax evasion. He was polite and well spoken with an air of calm to him. I couldn't imagine him bursting into a bank and ordering everyone to get down on the floor. 'I'm in for selling MDMA,' I told him. 'What, you were selling plywood?' he asked, a look of confusion spread across his face. 'No, that's MDF,' I explained. 'Death peddler!' he piped up, a tone of sudden realisation to his otherwise softly spoken voice. 'You're a death peddler! It's all drugs nowadays. Everyone's selling plywood to these smackheads and crackheads. Back in my day it was all armed robbers and safe crackers – now it's all scumbags.' According to his logic, I was obviously a less reputable class of criminal than he was. 'You wouldn't have had it back in my day,' he went on. 'I'm from the old school – we had morals back then.'

After I had explained to him that MDMA was not addictive and that it wasn't in the same league as crack or heroin, the unlikely armed robber seemed to soften up a little. 'You're still peddling death,' he told me. 'But you aren't as bad as some of the other drug scum, I suppose. Or the lowlives in here that are out robbing people's houses.' Listening to him, you would have thought that armed robbery was the most inoffensive crime that you could commit.

For the rest of the lesson I kept my head down and got on with my work. The neo-Nazi spent the day designing headed letter paper with a picture of Hitler in the background. 'I'm not saying that I agree with all of Hitler's views,' he told me. 'Drastic times call for drastic measures and it was what Germany needed at the time.' The Mancunian gangster remained quiet and the heroin dealer did a word search in the corner of the room.

At the end of the class, the teacher pulled me to one side. 'You need to be careful with Jim, that old guy,' he warned me. 'He's spent half his life in jail. They've got a picture of him up in Hull warning the staff about him. He's a dangerous man.' Jim hadn't seemed particularly aggressive or violent to me. He was passionately anti-drugs and seemed to think that armed robbery was the only acceptable form of crime; but, apart from that, he was fairly passive. I wondered what he had done to gain his fearsome reputation.

When I got back to the wing, I noticed that Jim was in a single cell. 'Why's he got a cell to himself?' I asked another inmate. 'He's high-risk,' he told me. 'He's not allowed a cellmate. They don't trust him to be locked up with someone else.' I was finding this hard to get my head around. He looked more like an accountant than a high-risk criminal.

The next time I was in the computer room, I tried to get to the bottom of why Jim was supposedly so dangerous. 'I've heard that they've got a picture of you up in Hull jail,' I told him. 'What's all that about?' He looked amused. 'Have they? I thought that was just a rumour!' It could well have been, as the teacher wasn't the most reliable source of information. He liked to exaggerate. 'What have you done that's so bad?' I asked him.

It turned out that most of Jim's crimes had been committed against the prison authorities. He had spent 25 years in prison and a good proportion of that time was served in the segregation unit. He recalled countless stories in which he had attacked various members of prison staff and he seemed to hate anyone who was in a position of power. 'They wouldn't normally even have me in a place like this,' he told me. 'Every other jail I've been in has been maximum-security. The screws in here aren't like they are in them places. They torture you – they had me in segregation for years on end. Can you imagine that?' The short stint that I'd spent on my own between cellmates had been bad enough. Still, he must have provoked them somehow.

'I certainly made it difficult for them if that's what you mean,' he grinned. 'One time they were moving me to another jail and I left an orange in my cell. I asked them if I could go back in and get it and they said no. I said I'm not going anywhere without my orange.' Jim was a man of principle. It didn't matter to him that it was a piece of fruit. It was an item of his property. 'In the end, six of them jumped all over me with batons and riot shields. When they had finally restrained me, I'd missed the transport and they had to keep me there for another three weeks. They made damn sure I had my orange with me the next time!'

Jim had caused havoc in every jail they put him in. He didn't like being told what to do and no amount of solitary confinement was going to make him change his mind. He raged against the system wherever he went. To his fellow prisoners, he was the nicest guy you could meet. To anyone in any slight position of power, he was their worst nightmare.

'All these prison guards think they have more morals than me,' he told me. 'They are murderers. When I was in maximum-security, they let a nonce hang himself a few doors down – he was on suicide watch. They should have been looking in every 15 minutes. We had a mock trial for them. We had someone play the defence, someone as the prosecution and another guy as the judge. In the end, we found them guilty and sentenced them to five minutes of raspberries.' He chuckled to himself. 'Can you imagine it? A bunch of hardened criminals blowing raspberries through the door! The screws were going mad!'

So was Jim's criminal activity a product of his anti-establishment mentality? Seemingly so. According to him, the government had made it so hard to live that crime was the only available option. There were only certain crimes that he would do. House burglaries and drug dealing were off limits. He made a clear distinction between crimes against a shop or a business and crimes against an individual. 'They get it all back on insurance,' he told me. 'If you rob a house, it's an invasion of privacy. If you rob a shop nobody really cares that much.'

So how did he justify the danger that he placed people in by waving a loaded gun in their face? 'I never put bullets in it,' he protested. 'I keep them on me for if the cops turn up – they don't mess about, so why should I?' He hated the police even more than he hated prison guards. 'So have you ever hurt anyone during a robbery?' I asked him. 'Nah,' he told me. 'I would never hurt an innocent person.' But he would kill a policeman. He had a strange way of looking at things.

'Right, time to go back to the wing,' the teacher told us. The neo-Nazi hurriedly finished printing off a picture of Hitler to put on his cell wall. The heroin dealer folded up his word search and put it in his pocket. I wondered what had driven Jim to a life of crime in the first place. He was very moralistic – it seemed strange that he made a living from doing hold-ups. He would have been more suited to an office job or working behind the desk of a library. As I walked back to the wing, I noticed a flock of birds gathering outside his window. They were fighting over a pile of crumbs that he had left out for them. I smiled to myself. It was in keeping with his kindly-old-man image – although not so much with his authority-hating, armed-robber persona.

That afternoon I decided to ask a few of the other inmates what they thought about Jim. He spent most of his time doing arts and crafts in his cell and rarely mixed with the rest of the wing. He would make colourfully painted pencil holders, using paintbrushes that he had stolen from the art department. Most of the other inmates spent their time gambling or trying to trade various items for drugs. I couldn't help but feel that he had good reason to keep to himself.

'He's a sound guy,' another prisoner told me, 'but get on his bad side and you will know about it! He's a big-time armed blagger [robber]. The police trail him whenever he's out of prison. He was an expert safe cracker back in the day.' It seemed that Jim's reputation was well known across the jail. 'He hates the cops,' another inmate chimed in. 'I heard that a copper had a restraining order against him 'cause he kept showing up at his house. He was sick of being followed by them so he turned the tables on them.' Everybody on the wing seemed to have a different story about Jim.

The next day, I plonked myself down in my usual spot next to the neo-Nazi. We were usually the first to arrive and he liked to get me on my own so that he could tell me his Hitler anecdotes without the black and Asian inmates hearing him. 'I've got nothing against the blacks or the Jews,' he told me. 'I just think Hitler would have got rid of the Pakis and the pikies if he was here today. And the Eastern Europeans too – all these Kosovans coming over here and taking our jobs . . .'

'Hi, Death Peddler!' Jim boomed in my ear. Thank God – he had come to save me from the Nazi. 'I saw you on the wing today. You were talking to a house burglar – what are you having it with people like that for?' If he had his way, only armed robbers and commercial burglars would be given the time of day by any of the other inmates. I tried to explain to him that drug dealers and house burglars made up 90 per cent of the prison population. 'You don't see me mixing with them scumbags, do you?' he retorted. He hung about with a drug smuggler, one step away from a dealer. It wasn't worth arguing with him, though – he was incredibly stubborn.

'I saw the birds outside your window,' I told him, trying to change the subject. 'Don't they wake you up in the morning?' He smiled. 'Well, I owe it to them. I hit a bird in my car once and didn't stop for it. Ever since then, I've looked after them and made sure they've had enough food.' The man who professed to keep a set of bullets handy in case he needed to shoot a police officer felt guilty because he had accidentally run over a bird.

A few hours into the lesson, one of the guards came in to ask if anyone had seen the missing paintbrushes from the art room. 'I've got them!' Jim bellowed from the other side of the classroom. She shot him a sarcastic smile. 'If they turn up, let me know. We've had some pots of paint go missing as well.' He chortled to himself. 'I'll be having the rest of them later,' he whispered to me.

Back on the wing, I tried to make sense of the day's events. Jim seemed to delight in his own eccentricity. He was a nonconformist – that was why he hated authority. It represented a conventional way of life, whereas he played by his own rules. 'Have you seen the birds outside the old man's window?' I asked my friend Tony, a house burglar whom Jim would no doubt have described as a 'scumbag'. 'Yeah, he likes his birds,' he told me. 'He's meant to have broken into a building to free a pigeon that was trapped in there once.' This was one of many Jim stories in circulation around the prison. It was difficult to separate the myth from the reality.

The next day, I was greeted in the usual manner. 'How's it going, Death Peddler?' he boomed. 'Not bad, Birdman,' I replied. 'But I saw you talking to a house burglar earlier.' Jim looked flustered. He had been talking to Willy, who was far worse than your average house burglar. Jim was probably completely oblivious of what he was in for. I would imagine that, if he'd found out some of the things that Willy had done, he would never talk to him again. 'Who was it?' Jim demanded. 'That's for me to know!' I told him. He frowned and his wrinkled brow crinkled up even more than it usually did. 'Well, if I find out who it is, I won't talk to them again!' He had reacted exactly as I predicted.

Jim spent the rest of the day telling me various anecdotes about his struggles against the system. His stories fell into two categories – things he had done to piss the guards off and things he had done to piss the police off. He recalled an incident in which he had caught onto an undercover agent following him home. 'I stopped off at a phone box to ring my girlfriend,' he told me. 'When I tried to put my money in, the coin got stuck. It's a scam – smackheads block up the chute where the money goes in so that they can collect it all at the end of the day.' It was only 20p but it was his 20p and he wanted it back. 'I was just heading home to get some tools so I could get my money out when this other fella walked into the phone box and pretended to make a call. I thought it was a bit strange, seeing as it wouldn't work for me. I came back with a screwdriver and prised my way in and there was only one coin in there, which was mine. He was trying to check who I had been ringing!'

It must have been a difficult existence being tailed whenever he was out of prison. 'You don't know the half,' he told me. 'My girlfriend is a solicitor and the cops keep putting pressure on her to leave me.' His life got more and more bizarre. He was an armed robber who was going out with a solicitor! 'They keep telling her how dangerous I am. We've been going out for years – I think she knows me better than they do!'

'Come on, time for rubdown,' the guard bellowed into the classroom. It was time for her to pat us down to make sure we didn't have any weapons on us. It seemed illogical that they did this at the end of the day. Surely they should have been trying to prevent us from bringing weapons *into* the classroom rather than smuggling them *out*. Besides, Jim had managed to steal half of the art room, so it wasn't exactly a thorough search.

Back on the wing, I began to wonder what Jim's girlfriend thought of his lifestyle. If she was a solicitor, she was no doubt middle-class and university-educated. Maybe she found it exciting dating a notorious armed robber – or perhaps she was tolerant of those aspects of his life. The fact that he spent most of his life in prison must have put a strain on things. He had told her parents that he was working away in Germany. If their relationship was ever going to progress, he would have to come clean to them about what he did for a living.

Just as I was pondering the complexities of Jim's love life, I heard him shouting angrily from the other side of the wing. I looked over and saw him locked in combat with Psycho Baz – the inmate who had kicked Wayne in the head. Jim's ear was gushing with blood and he was punching and kicking for all he was worth. Baz had a reputation for being a loose screw. He was a fan of using knives and wasn't the type of person it was wise to pick a fight with. I had to admire Jim's bravery.

Six burly prison guards came running over and hauled Jim and Baz to opposite corners of the wing. Baz had become increasingly aggressive over the last few weeks. Just days earlier, he had punched another inmate in the face for spilling gravy on his table at dinner.

For his part in the fight, Jim was taken to the segregation unit pending an adjudication. He was a little old to be getting into fistfights. He seemed to have given as good as he got, though. I just hoped that Baz wasn't planning a revenge attack. 'The other fella's got more to worry about,' Tony assured me. 'Jim knows some naughty people on the out – he's been in jail a long time. He knows a lot of faces.'

A few days later, Jim was back on the computers. He had a bandage on his ear but apart from that he was relatively unharmed. 'How's it going, Death Peddler?' came his standard greeting. 'Not bad, Birdman,' I replied. 'I saw your fight the other day – what was the deal with that?' It was better to ask him straight out than try to wheedle it out of him. 'He made a snide comment,' he told me. 'I didn't like him in the first place – he's a nasty piece of work.' Baz was the one person on the wing who made me feel unsafe, it had to be said. Everyone else needed a reason to attack you – he was liable to go off without warning.

The day of the adjudication came and Jim managed to get off with a few days of cell confinement. He had already spent some time in segregation and the prison officers saw no need to overreact to what was essentially a fairly minor altercation. Within no time at all, he was back on the course and making his usual death-peddling comments. 'He's a druggie like you, that Baz is!' he told me. 'Off his head. That's why he's always hitting people. He's been taking that plywood that you were selling.'

'Rubdown!' the guard shouted through. 'We've got

the drug dog here today.' Jim looked smug. He was as anti-drugs as it was possible to be – he had nothing to worry about. Everyone else looked worried. He was probably the only person in the room who didn't have drugs on him. Wraps of clingfilm were being inserted into body cavities right, left and centre.

The minute Jim stepped out of the door, the dog was on him. 'Get your dog under control!' he warned the screws. 'If it jumps up at me again I'm going to smack it!' It seemed that his kindness towards birds didn't extend to canines – especially when they were on the side of the prison authorities. For a highly trained drug dog, it had to be said that it was particularly bad at its job. It was accosting the one person who had never taken a single drug in his life.

The dog remained as boisterous as ever. It took a running leap at the old man and knocked his glasses case out of his hands. True to his word, he slapped it around the face with the back of his hand. 'The next time I'll wring its neck,' he told them. 'That's assaulting an officer!' the handler exclaimed. 'You'll be down the segregation for that!' The drug dogs were legally classed as prison officers. Attacking them was a serious offence.

'I'm not having this,' Jim ranted as we walked back across to the wing. 'If that dog's an officer then that was brutality! It assaulted me.' He hated screws, whether they had two legs or four. 'I'm going to ring the police on the prison phone,' he told me. 'I'm going to say I've just been attacked.'

He wasn't joking. Five minutes later, he had dialled

999 and told the police that the prison staff had assaulted him. They were duty-bound to investigate his claims. He was furious and determined to kick up as much of a fuss as he could. 'I'm going to say it was self-defence!' he ranted. 'I'm out in a few weeks so, if I can get my adjudication adjourned for long enough, I won't be here by the time they've decided what to do with me.'

If he had stuck to his plan, it might have worked. As it was, he went berserk and attacked the guards during the adjudication. He was hauled off to the segregation unit and made to spend the rest of his sentence in solitary confinement.

'How's Jim doing? I asked one of the segregation cleaners. I was missing him at education – I had no one to call me a death peddler and criticise me for selling drugs. 'He's not been eating and he's refusing to wash or shave,' he told me. 'He's got a big scraggly beard and he's lost a load of weight.' I was shocked. He was getting out soon – it would have been easier for him to have gone along with the system for the last few days of his sentence. He was too stubborn for his own good.

On the day of Jim's release, he took one last stand against the authorities. 'I'm going out naked,' he told them, 'and I'm going to say you chucked me out without any clothes.' He wasn't going to let them get away with the injustice they had inflicted upon him. The guards were panicking. They couldn't throw him out without any clothes on but, at the same time, it was illegal to hold him past his release date.

After a good half an hour of bargaining, the prison

staff managed to get Jim to wear a pair of prison-issue boxer shorts. They told him that, if he went out completely naked, the police would be waiting outside the prison gates and he would be promptly rearrested. It was his final act of rebellion. The other prisoners were talking about his defiance for weeks – in their eyes he was a hero. He was a strange old man but there was something endearing about his awkwardness. Out of all the people I met during my sentence, he was the one who would stick in my mind. He was willing to walk down the street butt naked to get one over on the authorities.

To Jim, doing crime was a way of sticking it to the system. Whereas the current generation stole to feed their habits, he stole to rebel. For him, the worst possible fate was to lose face. He was a man of principles – no matter how misguided those principles were. To the police and the prison guards, he was their worst nightmare. To me, he was a slightly eccentric, grey-haired old man who walked around the wing in his dressing gown.

CHAPTER 8
MALONEY

Not everybody I met in prison was a career criminal. Some had made a single mistake that had cost them the rest of their lives. A good proportion of the lifers' wing was like that: people who were for the most part good but who had succumbed to a moment of uncharacteristic madness. Some of them had never experienced adulthood outside a cell. They were still paying for what they had done as teenagers, and they had been locked away ever since. Youthful rage and impulsiveness had stripped them of their formative years and they would never get them back. Everyone has their triggers and anyone can reach breaking point, given the right amount of pressure. These people were a living testament to this.

It was a trigger that had cost Maloney the past 14 years of his life – the trigger of a sawn-off shotgun. He hadn't had the best start in life. His parents had split up when he was in his early teens and his brother took exception to his mum's new boyfriend and killed him. To say that he came from a broken home would be putting it mildly. He grew up in a deprived part of Leeds called Cottingley – a large area consisting entirely of council housing. Several of his older brothers were in and out of prison and he was no stranger to crime. However, it was not until he reached the age of 14 that he became actively involved in these activities, as opposed to passively observing the felonies of others.

Maloney was very protective of his younger sister. He was not the type of person to stand back and watch someone take advantage of her. The stories that were circulating around the estate made him increasingly anxious. She was only 13 – still a child. There were rumours that she was in a relationship with a 30-year-old man. If he'd so much as laid a finger on her, he'd kill him. He had questions that needed answering straightaway. He and she were going to have some serious words.

'It's true!' his sister told him, 'but it's not like you think – we're in love!' Maloney couldn't believe what he was hearing. A grown man was sleeping with a 13-year-old girl and, to top it off, he was a Muslim. He'd read in the tabloids how they treated their women and he was fuming. This was child abuse. He was a nonce – and he was noncing on his sister. There was only one thing for it. He would have to pay this man a visit.

Although he had never used a gun before, Maloney was streetwise and knew where to get hold of one at a moment's notice. He couldn't have a paedophile grooming his sister and getting away with it – something had to be done. Within the hour, he had a shiny new shotgun laid out in front of him. He didn't have any ammunition but he could still give that filthy paedo a good scare and make sure he never came near his sister again.

'In a way, I was showing off,' Maloney told me. 'I didn't have to get the gun. I could have just handled it with my fists but I wanted to look big.' His voice was choked with regret and he didn't seem like the same person he had been all that time ago. He was one of the more grounded people I met during my time behind bars and seemed to have come on in leaps and bounds since he had first got locked up. 'The nonce was working at the post office, so I went to see him at his work. I ended up getting a bit overhyped and did something stupid.'

'Put the money in the bag!' What was he doing? This wasn't part of the plan. This was armed robbery. He could get into serious trouble. 'I want all the spirits and cigarettes as well. Put them in there now or I'll blow your head off.' If this came on top, he could be looking at a very long stretch indeed. 'You dirty paedo – get in the van!' Where was he even going to take him? Things had already gone horribly too far and he was fully aware of it, but he ploughed on regardless. The adrenaline had gone to his head and he couldn't back down now. Panic set in. He didn't have anywhere to take him apart from back to his house in Cottingley. He would have to leave him in the spare room until he decided what he was going to do with him. 'Put this over your eyes!' he shouted, handing a piece of torn cloth over to the terrified postal worker for him to use as a blindfold. He couldn't have him seeing where he lived. As he pulled up on his street, he felt a tight knot of dread forming deep in his stomach. He was now a kidnapper. Where was this all going to end?

Still no clearer as to what to do with his newly acquired prisoner, Maloney tied him to the radiator and bound his arms and legs together to stop him from running away. 'You dirty, noncy little paedo!' he shouted. 'You leave little girls alone from now on, do you hear me?' The man nodded. He would do whatever he said so long as it meant that he could get out of there alive.

A week later, the nonce was still there. He was given food and water and allowed out to use the toilet. He was also punched, kicked and threatened on a regular basis. Large purple bruises covered his body and he was bleeding. Maloney didn't want a murder charge hanging over him – they already had one lifer in the family and didn't need another one. It was time to let him go. He drove back to the post office and left the badly beaten worker slumped against the front entrance.

'I don't know what I was thinking!' he told me. 'It was crazy!' He refused to disclose exactly how much he had gained from the robbery but the word on the wing was that it was £7,000 in cash and a few thousand pounds more from the spirits and cigarettes. This was not a bad amount, but still not worth risking his freedom over. There were easier crimes to get away with.

'A few weeks later I had the 5-0 [police] knocking at my door. Someone had grassed me up and I was in deep shit.' Maloney got five years and nine months for armed robbery, four years and nine months for aggravated vehicle taking and four years for kidnap. Seeing that these were all fairly serious crimes, they could not run concurrently. He was looking at a total of 14 years and 6 months – half a year short of a life sentence.

Due to his age, Maloney started his sentence in a secure unit and then progressed on to a young offenders' institution and then finally to an adult jail. Institutions quickly became his life. Like many prisoners who are doing long sentences, he became infatuated with the gym. Building his body up was the only way he could use his time productively. 'I went from 10 stone to 16 stone,' he told me. There was a rumour on the wing that he had been using steroids, but, regardless of his methods, it had to be said he was in good shape. His arms were like tree trunks and he looked as strong as an ox.

There is a saying in jail that doing time is easy until something goes wrong on the outside. Maloney could vouch for this. The worst thing about his whole sentence was the fact that his brother had died while he was locked up. He talked about it endlessly and was visibly traumatised by the whole affair. 'I wish I'd been out there to grieve with my family,' he told me. I really felt for him. It must have been awful for such a tragedy to happen while he was still in prison, knowing that he would have to wait until his next visit to find out the full details. Life behind bars was no easy ride.

'The worst thing about it was that I got recalled straightaway when I got released. I'd been in nine and a half years before they let me out on licence and I was back in after five months.' This must have been terrible. Prisoners usually serve a proportion of their sentence in custody and then the rest of it on licence. During this period, the offender must report regularly to their probation officer and abide by a strict set of rules that vary from person to person. In Maloney's case, he was to remain in a bail hostel between the hours of 10pm and 8am.

'I was late back.' He hung his head in shame. 'It was ten past ten. They probably wouldn't have breached me just for that, but they were trying to say I was part of a gang as well because I always had a big group of people round at the hostel. It was bollocks though: I've just got a big family. I've got seven brothers and three sisters.' This was quite an assumption to make on their part, although breaking his curfew was reason alone to send him back to prison. 'They were bastards at the hostel – I had a bit of cash on me and they tried to say it was drug money.' In some people's eyes it is a case of once a criminal, always a criminal.

Perhaps the most tragic part of Maloney's story was that his sister stayed with the postal worker despite everything that had happened. She is now living with him and he is the father of her children. Maloney had sacrificed his freedom for nothing. 'I won't even speak to her now,' he told me. 'As far as I'm concerned, I have no sister.' I could feel the pain and betrayal in his voice as he spoke. 'I'm going to spend a lot more time with the rest of my family when I get out, though. I need to mourn my brother's death properly with them all around me. We are a close family and I feel like I let them down by not being there.'

'So you won't be making the same mistake again?' I asked.

'No way!' he told me. 'I never want to come back here again. I've done enough jail in this lifetime. I want to be a better person when I get out.' At least some good had come of all of this in that it had given him the motivation to try hard to better himself. I wondered how he would cope in the outside world. A lot must have changed since he was last out there. He had only had five months of freedom in the past fourteen years and most of that was spent in a bail hostel. How would he relate to law-abiding citizens after spending so much time locked up? Criminals had been his only peers for over a decade. It must have had an influence on the way he thought and behaved. I wished him luck. He deserved a life, and prison was no life at all.

Time passed and it was getting close to the day of Maloney's release. He looked worried. 'Do you think I'm going bald?' he asked me. 'I don't want everyone to look at me when I get out and think, What the hell's happened to your hair?' I assured him that he still had plenty of hair and that no one would think anything of the sort. 'Do you think people will notice the weight I've put on? I want them to look at me and see the work I've done in the gym!' People would notice. Muscles bulged from every inch of his body – he could have lifted me up and bench-pressed me without breaking sweat. 'They will see it,' I told him.

Finally his release date came. 'Maloney!' boomed the voice of a burly male prison guard. 'Home time!' His day had come. It was time to go back into society. He looked terrified. I shook his hand. 'You'll be fine,' I said, trying to calm him down a bit. At long last he could return to the civilised world – a world where he had once belonged but was now unsure about. It was time for him to make up for all the years he had lost.

CHAPTER 9

SMALLS

Maloney was one of the few inmates from Leeds who had not come from one of six areas. These were Beeston (home of the 7/7 London bombers), Armley, Gipton, East End Park, Seacroft (the city's largest council estate) and Chapeltown – where all of the black inmates I met had come from.

Chapeltown differs from the other crime hotspots within the city in that there are large amounts of automatic weapons there and people are willing to shoot to kill. Whereas criminals in Seacroft and Gipton often use guns, it is normally only for intimidation, and it is rare for people to actually pull the trigger. The media have blamed Chapeltown's recent rise in gun crime on Yardies and other black immigrants. Smalls knew better than this. It was people like him that had kept the crime rate there consistently high – people who were born and raised there. Sure, there were a few immigrants involved in certain things as well, but a grafter was a grafter regardless of nationality. Jamaican, African, white, black British – crime has no race, creed or country of origin.

Growing up in the heart of the red-light district, it was hard to escape the gritty realities of inner-city life. Prostitutes walked the streets and there was a constant rabble of crackheads roaming the area trying to score drugs. Life was far from pretty. Smalls's environment would go on to define him and he would soon become a part of the problem.

After being expelled from school for fighting, he quickly grew bored of sitting around and doing nothing. What was the point in twiddling his thumbs waiting to find a new school when there was a whole world of vice for him to explore? He knew a few older youths in the area who were making a name for themselves as burglars and decided to tag along with them. What they were doing was far more exciting than school.

'We weren't doing no sneak-thieves,' Smalls explained. 'We were kicking doors off with hammers and crowbars and filling bags up with people's jewellery in front of them. Why sneak about when you've got tools on you?' This negated the need for any particular skill or finesse. He was getting what he wanted by sheer brute force – no subtlety involved. 'What if someone tried to stop you?' I asked him. He laughed. 'No one ever did.'

At 14 Smalls had his first run-in with the law. They had found his fingerprints in one of the houses he had robbed. He was charged with aggravated burglary and placed on an eight o'clock curfew. This did nothing to deter him. It merely caused him to shift from burglary to drug dealing, as there was less chance of detection. He bought a bag of crack and a bag of heroin and set about finding some customers.

By the age of 18, Smalls was making a lot of money. His trainers were worth more than some people's entire wardrobes were and he was moving drugs almost as fast as he could buy them. Selling drugs in Chapeltown was a risky business. Dealers in the area were constantly getting shot and stabbed, so he had to have his gun on him at all times.

With drugs came violence. Smalls's first jail sentence was for the serious charge of kidnap. He was accused of abducting an Asian male, pistol-whipping him and shooting him in the legs. He claimed in court that, although he had abducted him, it was someone else who had shot him. As there was insufficient evidence to prove otherwise, this story ensured that he was charged only with the abduction. 'I told them that I snatched him to take him to my bredrin [friend] who wanted to make him sell drugs for him.' This didn't seem very plausible. People being forced into selling drugs is something of an urban myth – I have never heard of it in real life. 'I'm glad he got shot, though,' he smiled. 'He kept ringing my wifey up on some stalking shit. He deserved to get popped. Still, it wasn't me that did it.' I suspected otherwise. His facial expressions were telling a different story altogether.

'He'd been one of my close friends before it all

happened,' Smalls explained. 'I was always buying him clothes, chains, whatever he wanted. It's a shame he had to get done in.' He didn't sound overly sincere. 'He got his eye and his lip all bust up and I guess he'll be walking with a limp from now on,' he smiled.

'Jail was like a school for criminals.' This was in line with what everyone else had said. 'I got transferred to nine different jails on suspicion of selling drugs. If I'd been selling drugs in that many different jails, I would have made around . . . oh, I dunno, around 26 grand?' This was over a period of two years. 'Most people in jail sell smack 'cause that's where the money is. If people don't pay, you can easily pay someone else a few bags to slash them.' And so his drugs empire had continued from behind bars.

When he got out, Smalls went straight back to what he had done before. Within a few weeks, he had rebuilt his customer base and it was as if he'd never been away. He was more cautious now, though. Instead of keeping his gun on him, he left it in the care of a 16-year-old girl on the Wyther Park estate in Bramley. She had become infatuated with him and was enthralled by his bad-boy image. She was willing to risk her freedom for him and kept his sub-machine-gun with silencer and infrared sight hidden in the back of her wardrobe.

Smalls's gun was a 9mm black starting pistol with the barrel removed and a rifle barrel inserted in its place. It had been modified to make it automatic and fell within the category of what was commonly referred to as 'spray and pray' – a term used to describe weapons so powerful that they are almost impossible to aim. It was not your standard firearm – it was capable of doing some serious damage.

One day he was drinking with the 16-year-old and two of his white friends from Bramley when the police came over to their table. It turned out that two men matching his friends' descriptions had committed a street robbery earlier that night. All four of them were taken down to the cells for questioning. They were released without charge but the fact that the 16-year-old had been arrested aroused the suspicion of her mother, who had suspected for some time that something had been going on. A search of her daughter's bedroom quickly uncovered the gun along with two clips (one standard and one extended) and a case of hollow-tip bullets. She drove straight down to the police station and handed them in.

The 16-year-old was immediately placed on witness protection and told that, unless she was willing to testify against Smalls, she would be charged with firearm possession and remanded in custody. She grudgingly agreed to give evidence, knowing that this decision would put her life in severe danger. Smalls was given bail to attend court in a few weeks' time but he had no intention of ever doing so. He chose instead to skip court and hide out at the house of one of his friends.

'When they finally found me they came with helicopters and an armed response unit,' he told me. 'I had some drugs on me, so I plugged them, but I forgot I had more in my jacket pocket and some money as well.'

He was caught with £1,500 and a small amount of crack and heroin and sentenced to three years in prison. During this time, his fingerprints were found on the gun case and he was given an additional seven years.

'What did you need a sub-machine-gun for?' I asked him. 'Would you have used it on anyone?' I suspected I already knew the answer to this one. 'Yeah, no doubt,' he replied. 'You see this?' he said, rolling up his trouser leg to reveal a large bullet hole in his left leg. 'That's a gunshot wound. If people are willing to do it to me, I've got to be willing to go one step further and shoot their mum in her leg.' This was an attitude I was slowly becoming accustomed to. 'But it's not their mum that's done it to you,' I replied, hardly bothering to even argue. 'Yeah, but if you aren't ruthless, people will take you for a chief [fool]. I've had someone in my family kidnapped before and I knew that they were bluffing so I said, "Do it, then." They did nothing. If it's war, you have to be prepared to go all out.' I was glad I didn't move in the same circles as he did.

Towards the back of Smalls's cell stood a statue of Buddha surrounded by incense sticks. It seemed strangely out of place. After hearing all his stories of gun slinging and drug dealing, seeing a symbol of peace in his living quarters was unexpected to say the least. 'I'm a Buddhist,' he explained, catching my gaze and guessing my train of thought. 'The meditation helps me to relax.' I wondered how this fitted in with his Sopranos-type lifestyle. 'Will it make you less violent when you get out, then?' I asked him. 'Well . . .' he grinned. 'I might do less premeditated violence, but if it's spur-of-the-moment then it's going to happen anyway.' At least this was an improvement. Perhaps the statue represented the fact that he was searching for peace but was as yet unable to achieve it.

I wondered just how many people like Smalls there were on Britain's streets. He was the second person I'd heard talk about shooting people's mums. This was clearly a fairly common threat to make. It was an unwritten rule that, if someone couldn't get to their intended target, it was acceptable for them to go after their nearest and dearest. I had assumed that England was a safe place to live but I had only seen things from a sheltered, middle-class perspective. There was a world that, until now, I had known very little about. A world where guns and ammunition meant absolute power.

CHAPTER 10
SULLY

If guns meant power, then Sully was the dispenser of this power. His previous charge was one of conspiracy to supply firearms and he had a lengthy history of illegal activity. The strangest thing was that he actually seemed like a genuinely nice guy. Although he was a little rough around the edges, he came across as warm and friendly with no hint of malevolence. I really couldn't picture him selling guns, but his criminal record told a different story.

Sully came from Ravenscliffe, perhaps best known for the disturbances there during the Bradford riots. Burnt-out cars littered the streets and boarded-up houses provided homes for junkies and glue sniffers. It was one of Bradford's many dumping grounds. 'It wasn't hard growing up there, though,' he told me. 'A lot of people from these areas like to say they've had it bad but if you've grown up there and you know everyone it's alright. It's all you know, really.'

Despite his deprived surroundings, Sully retained a fairly upbeat perspective on life. Rather than feel sorry for himself, he kept his head down and got on with his sentence. He was always asking me how I was getting on and was very polite and courteous for an arms dealer. How had someone like this got involved in selling firearms? It had all started with weed.

'I was smoking an ounce a day,' he explained. This is a phenomenal amount. It meant that he was spending in excess of £800 a week on a drug that isn't even physically addictive. This is more than some heroin addicts spend a week on smack. 'I could just about afford it, but then when I was 16 I got a £400 fine for driving without a licence.' He shouldn't have even been driving a car at that age. 'That's what made me realise I was going to have to start doing crime or stop smoking weed. And there was no way I was going to stop smoking the weed!' Sully could already drive, so the logical crime for him to get involved in was car theft. He knew of a gang in the city who specialised in stealing high-performance sports cars and set about gaining their favour. Impressed by his driving skills, they were soon happy to have him on board.

There were 14 members of the gang in all – roughly half of them were Asian and the other half were white. Ten of them were from Bradford, two were from Dewsbury, one was from Pudsey and one was from the Batley Carr estate in nearby Batley. None of the Asian members stole any of the cars themselves – they were all fences. Car theft is a very white crime and during my time behind bars I encountered very few black or Asian TWOCers.

Sully was thought to be earning a good two grand a night. He was going after Porsches, Lotuses, Audis and Mercedes. He would acquire the keys by doing 'tea-timers' – sneaking into houses while the occupants were eating their tea. He checked the obvious places for people's car keys and then drove their cars away while they were obliviously tucking into their meals. 'Fruit bowls – they were a standard one,' he told me. 'Otherwise they would be on the table, in the kitchen drawer or in a handbag.' He would either sneak in through an unlocked door or use a maul grip to prise out the lock.

The gang could have made a lot more money if they'd had better fences: they were selling vehicles worth £50,000 for a thousand pounds or less. Not all of them shared Sully's expertise at driving, either. One thief attempted to steal a £48,000 Maserati sports car only to find he was unable to work the complicated paddle-shift gears. He managed to jump out of the car just in time as it spun wildly out of control. The owner came out onto his driveway to see what all the noise was about and could only stand and stare as his expensive sports car careered into his expensive home. The collision caused £1,700 worth of damage to the Maserati and, during the commotion, another gang member drove away in his Mercedes.

'You seem like you've got a conscience, unlike some people in here,' I told him. 'Don't you feel bad for taking other people's cars?' Sully looked defensive. 'Well, people have got insurance, haven't they? It's not like they don't get the money back. They just have the inconvenience of not having the car for a few days.' This was a commonly held belief among car thieves. It completely ignored the fact that the owner's insurance costs would go through the roof and, also, how did he think the homeowners would feel knowing that someone had been sneaking around in their house while they were still in it? 'If they saw someone else getting their house burgled, do you think they'd do anything about it?' he asked. Maybe, maybe not but that was beside the point. They still didn't deserve having their car stolen or their privacy invaded like this. He had a very strange way of justifying his actions. 'I do know what it feels like,' he told me. 'I've had cars taken off me by police that they thought were TWOCed before.' It was hardly the same thing. 'I grafted hard to get them, so it's pretty similar.' I shook my head in disbelief.

'Another way I "could" have made money was from selling weed,' he told me. 'I'm not saying that I did but . . . use your imagination.' If he was smoking an ounce a day it made sense for him to have bought in bulk and sold some on. If he had got to the point where he was selling enough weed to fund his own habit, virtually all the money he got from the cars would have been disposable income. The only things he really spent his cash on were weed, clothes, beer and food.

There was only so much to be earned from selling soft drugs. Sully began to notice that certain members of the gang were earning significant amounts from dealing heroin. 'When I reached 17, I started wanting the big money. I can't tell you what I did to get it but you can probably guess.' It didn't take a rocket scientist. 'Let's put it this way. You could earn £600 a day from selling gear – that's a lot of cash for making a few drop-offs every day.'

Between them, Sully and his friends were making a killing from the cars alone. Selling drugs was the icing on the cake. Even though they were selling the sports cars at a mere fraction of their actual value, they were still making a substantial profit. There had been no sign of the police sniffing around and some of the members had discovered that they could make a fair bit on the side from selling guns. Two guys called Andy and Danny kept coming back for more weapons and it was a bit of extra cash every now and again. 'You can get a gun within the hour in Ravenscliffe if you really need one,' Sully explained. 'They are never really that far away.' They didn't seem to be that far away wherever you were, from what I had heard.

'A few different people sorted them out. This guy Mahmoud got them a Colt .38 and I sold them a French double-barrel shotgun. I hooked them up with one of my mates who sold them a few bits as well. I think he got them a Beretta, a Glock and a starter pistol.' This was a big mistake. The first rule of selling any contraband items is never sell to anyone you don't know personally. Danny and Andy turned out to be PC Danny and PC Andy.

Sully got a total of eight years for conspiracy to burgle and conspiracy to supply firearms. He was given the harshest sentence of the whole gang, despite the fact that one of them was caught selling heroin and cocaine as well. It was his first prison sentence and it was a long one. Not long enough, though, as almost as soon as he was released on licence he was recalled to jail for committing a further offence.

'I needed a new front end for this Audi convertible I'd crashed,' he told me. 'I went out grafting to see if I could find one and while I was there, I saw another car that I liked.' All he had to do was sneak into the house and get the keys and it was his. His friend kept lookout while he took the lock out and snuck in through the front door. The first thing that caught his eye was a large plasma television. 'I'll have that!' he thought. He was just picking it up when he heard a shrill, high-pitched whistle from outside – the signal that something was up. He ran out of the house to see a police helicopter hovering overhead. Oh, shit! He would have to get out of there – and fast. He jumped into a nearby car and slammed his foot down on the accelerator.

After an hour-long chase, Sully crashed into a lamppost, dived out of the car and tried to escape on foot. He would perhaps have made it, had he not run straight into a barbed-wire fence. 'It didn't half hurt,' he told me. 'I got tangled up and couldn't get away. I got four and a half years for burglary and TWOC, to run concurrent with the licence-recall time for the firearms.'

'Do you think you'll nick any more cars when you get out, then?' I asked – my usual line of questioning at this point in the proceedings. 'Nah,' he told me. 'I've got a kid now and my baby mother wouldn't approve. Plus, there's no point, really. I've got my own fully mortgaged house, so I don't need to do crime now.' It would have been easy to pass Sully off as just another heartless villain, but I felt that he was merely thoughtless as opposed to truly wicked. He had a set of ill-thought-out excuses that he honestly believed made it OK for him to steal other people's things. Perhaps if he were to have his own house burgled, he would understand the suffering that he had exposed other people to. Had any of his friends or family had their house broken into or their car stolen? 'Yeah,' he replied. 'But that was nothing to do with me. We don't steal from our own in Ravenscliffe. Some estates do, but not round us.' I suppose that made it OK, then. He seemed to have no concept of what I was even getting at.

'I've got a few years ahead of me to think about what I've done,' Sully told me. His baby daughter would be at school by the time he got out. The only time she would see her father would be in the visiting room, surrounded by prison guards. Regardless of his motivation, it was good for all concerned that he had decided to go straight. I hoped he would stick to this decision and not be tempted to go back to his old ways. If not for his sake, then for his daughter's.

CHAPTER 11
WINGY

Whereas Sully was part of a highly organised criminal gang, there were numerous inmates who worked at much lower levels of sophistication. Those who were in and out of jail were looked upon with scorn by the other prisoners – not because of their inability to go straight but because they kept getting caught.

Of all of the habitual offenders that I met, Wingy was the most persistent. He was a car thief and house burglar – a low-level criminal. Although he had been involved in crime from an early age he had never quite got the hang of getting away with it. He was the wing's scapegoat. Whenever the other inmates had a bad day, they would victimise him to make themselves feel better. Heroin addicts would walk past and call him a smackhead. They were either in denial about their own addictions or saw him as a worse class of addict, even though he had managed to kick his heroin habit shortly after coming into the jail. To them, he would always be a junkie. He was passive and placid – an easy target. 'What are you talking to Wingy for?' the other prisoners would ask me. 'He's a worthless debt-head.'

True, he may have been a debt-head, but Wingy was also laid back and good company. He subscribed to the same bravado-driven ethos as the other cons but seemed to do so in a more half-hearted way. When the other inmates talked about grasses and informers, they had genuine hate in their eyes. When he spoke about them, it was as if he was toeing the party line. He was a half-hearted criminal – he did crime because it was all he knew, rather than out of malice.

Having managed to get himself off heroin, Wingy had eventually succumbed to its equally seductive cousin – Subutex. Half the wing were self-confessed 'Subby-heads', but he was the only one given a hard time for it. 'It's because he's always in debt,' my cellmate told me. Half of the wing were in debt. He was nothing out of the ordinary. It was the way that he went about paying his debts off that attracted condemnation. He would go around begging other inmates for items he could trade for drugs. 'Can I have a tin of tuna? I'm starving,' he would ask. The next minute, he'd be trying to trade it for a milligram of Subutex.

Wingy owed tobacco to one of the Asian drug dealers on another wing. He had owed it for some time and rumours were beginning to circulate that the Asian prisoners were going to attack him. The other inmates gathered around him in mock concern. 'You have to stick up for yourself,' they told him. 'You should make a shiv and go out onto the yard – tell them you aren't gonna pay!' They were trying to get him to start a fight so they could watch and feed off the violence. They didn't care about defending his pride – they just wanted to see someone get hurt.

That week, various Asian prisoners came to the wing, shouting threats through the bars. Wingy was terrified. 'My granddad always used to tell me not to settle things with violence,' he told me. 'I'm going to keep off the yard for a while.' This was another source of amusement for his tormentors. 'You'll be getting a ship out soon,' they told him. 'You'll be debted up to everyone in the prison and won't have the balls to do anything about it.' It must have been depressing knowing that he was confined to the wing for the rest of his time inside. His world had been cut in half. Yard time was the only time he got to go outside.

The next time I saw Wingy, he had slash marks up and down his wrists. It was his way of coping with things. You would have thought that the other prisoners would have eased up on him in light of what they had driven him to but they treated him exactly the same as before. They still mocked him every time he came past their cells. They drew a picture of a tap with his name written above it and stuck it on his cell door. 'Tapping' is jail slang for begging or scrounging. To them, he was a figure of fun and existed solely for their amusement.

The next day, Wingy was nowhere to be seen. He had refused to go to his cell, so that the wing staff would send him to the segregation unit. His debts had got too much for him to take. This way, he would be moved to another prison where he could start afresh – or so he thought. The screws had different ideas. There was still one wing where he didn't owe anyone any tobacco. 'You're off to E Unit,' they told him.

E Unit was nicknamed 'the notorious E Unit'. It was the roughest wing in the prison. Inmates were getting taxed right, left and centre and there were 'pad rushers' – gangs of prisoners that would run into people's cells and snatch their belongings. Our wing was fairly tame in comparison – if he couldn't survive there, he would have a bad time over on E Unit.

Within weeks of his transfer, the word spread that Wingy was in the segregation unit. He had got himself debted up yet again and the dealers on E Unit didn't beat about the bush. If they didn't get paid immediately, they started issuing threats. 'There's people saying they're going to run over and bang him when he's getting released,' another prisoner told me. There were inmates all over the prison who were looking to do him in, and it must have been scary for him.

A few days later, I was walking around the yard with my friends when I noticed a cloud of black smoke billowing out of the segregation unit. My first thought was that someone had set fire to it to try to get to Wingy. 'Back to your cells!' the guards bellowed. Whenever anything out of the ordinary happened, we were ushered back to our wings and locked up. 'What's happened?' I asked one of the screws. 'It's Wingy,' he told me. 'He's gone and set himself on fire.'

The rest of the wing were completely unfazed. People regularly set themselves alight in British prisons – it is one of the most popular forms of self-harm. The other inmates had seen it all before and were desensitised to it. 'We're still going to do him in if we see him on the way out,' an Asian prisoner told me. These were ruthless people. They didn't care how much pain Wingy was in – they wanted what he owed to them and they were determined to get it.

Fortunately for Wingy, his release went without a hitch. It was the end of his ordeal – although I couldn't help feeling that, once he had been set free, he might switch back from Subutex to heroin. I had never heard of anyone selling 'Subbies' in the outside world and wondered if they were even that readily available.

As it happened, Wingy was able to carry on taking Subutex just as he had done before – the week after he was released, he was remanded on another charge. 'If it's so hard for him in here then why does he carry on doing crime?' his former cellmate asked me. He had a very good point. Wingy had cut himself and set himself on fire because of what had happened on his sentence but yet here he was – back inside. I was beginning to see why all the other prisoners took his cries for help with a pinch of salt.

Wingy was a prime example of a man who was unhappy with his life but too apathetic to change it.

LOWLIFE

Crime was all he knew – he hated prison but he came back time after time. He had no qualifications and a criminal record – there weren't many other options available to him. It was either work at Burger King or rob and steal for a living. Drugs and self-harm were his only form of escape. Until he could find a legitimate source of income, he would remain unhappy for the rest of his life.

CHAPTER 12

JOHNNY

The worst thing that can happen during a jail sentence is for someone on the outside to die. The passing of a loved one is always a traumatic event but it is ten times worse when you are stuck behind bars. Those who have elderly or terminally ill relatives live in constant uncertainty. Unless they have regular visits or save enough money to spend on the prison phones, they are left completely in the dark.

Johnny's mum was dying of cancer. It was little wonder he had started taking heroin. She was all he had. 'When I get out of here, I'll be homeless,' he told me. 'I usually stay at hers but she hasn't got that long left.' It was hard not to feel sorry for him. He was a professional house burglar and deserved his time inside, but, at the same time, the knowledge that his mother was approaching her last breaths while he was locked away must have been unbearable. The rest of the wing were sympathetic towards his plight. Many of them had elderly relatives too. Johnny drowned his sorrows by smoking smack and taking Subutex; he was one of the biggest heroin addicts in the prison. He was pale and gaunt with a large, dark patch around each eye. Drugs and grief had taken their toll. He looked as if he was at death's door himself.

In theory, it should be impossible for a prisoner to take heroin and remain undetected by the prison guards. We were on the voluntary drug-testing wing, which meant that we were regularly tested for a variety of different substances. It was supposedly a drug-free wing but the reality couldn't have been further from that. There were a couple of simple ways to get round the tests. The first was to drink lots of water so that the sample would be too diluted to draw any conclusions from. The second involved concealing a plastic bag filled with somebody else's urine and puncturing it into the sample container. The downside to this method was that the prisoner taking the test would end up covered in somebody else's piss.

Johnny had his own method for avoiding the tests. He would cut his finger with a razor blade and trickle blood into the container. When the guards asked him what was happening, he told them that blood came out whenever he tried to go to the toilet. They couldn't force him to urinate if he had a medical condition that prevented him from doing so. He managed to effectively render himself immune to all future drug tests.

Finally, Johnny's mother passed away. He was devastated. She had loved him and supported him despite his life of crime. 'What am I going to do now?' he whimpered. Without her, he was effectively homeless. He had nowhere to go when he got out of prison. He had no one to send him any money either, which meant he would be unable to buy any more drugs. 'I wonder whether they'll let me out to go to the funeral,' he pondered. It would have been inhumane of them not to. He needed to be with the rest of his family – it was the only way that he could properly mourn her passing.

Later that week, the news arrived that Johnny would be allowed out to attend the funeral under the supervision of prison guards. It was known as a 'release on temporary licence' or 'rottle' in prisoners' slang. 'It's better than nothing,' he told me. 'I'd rather go on my own but at least it'll get me out of this place for the day.' It must have been embarrassing turning up at church surrounded by prison guards. Still, he got a chance to see his relatives and pay his last respects to his mother.

The day of the funeral arrived and Johnny made himself as presentable as possible. He gelled his hair and put on a shirt and a pair of smart dark-blue jeans. 'Come on, Johnny,' the guard said, ushering him out of his cell. 'Time to go.' As he walked through the gates, I wondered how he would feel when he got back on the wing. He would need a lot of moral support and most of it would no doubt come from his smack pipe. The other inmates would be sympathetic but there was only so much that they could do. He had suffered a tremendous loss and nothing anyone could say or do would bring his mother back.

'What was it like?' I asked him, as he came back through the gates. He looked strangely upbeat and cheery. 'It was good,' he told me. 'It went well.' He seemed a lot perkier than he had been over the last few days. Perhaps the chance to get off the wing for a while had done him good. His cheeks were rosy and he had a definite spring in his step.

'What's up with Johnny?' I asked my cellmate later that day. 'He's in a good mood, isn't he?' He gave me a knowing grin. 'All I'm saying is there's a lot more brown on the wing since his rottle.' Was he implying that Johnny had picked up a batch of heroin during his mother's funeral? Surely that would have been the last thing on his mind. And wasn't he under supervision? But, then again, he was an addict. Heroin was the most important thing in his world and everything else paled in comparison.

The next day, there were inmates selling their belongings right, left and centre. 'I'll give you these trousers for a pack of burn,' a toothless smackhead propositioned me. It certainly seemed as if somebody had brought in a large amount of heroin. The word on the wing was that Johnny had met a contact in a public toilet cubicle and he had passed him a lump of smack. He had quickly plugged it up his arse using his spit as a lubricant and walked out as if nothing had happened.

Later that evening, the guards raided Johnny's cell. They had received an anonymous tip-off that he was dealing Class A drugs. Although they didn't find anything, he was removed from the wing as a precautionary measure. It was starting to seem as if the rumours about him were true.

'Did you hear about Johnny?' I asked Big Issue, a well-known smackhead, as we ate our breakfast the following morning. Big Issue was one of the biggest drug users on the wing. He'd got his name from the fact that he looked like a tramp – a result of years of injecting smack. If anyone knew whether the stories were based in reality, it would be him. 'Yeah,' he grinned, his black and yellow teeth displaying numerous cavities. 'Good job I got my gear off him before he went.'

So it was true – Johnny had used his mother's funeral as an opportunity to buy drugs. In doing so he lost all sympathy from the other prisoners on the unit. 'He's a scumbag,' one of the other smackheads told me. 'That's the last thing I would be thinking of if my mum had just died.' The truth of the matter was that heroin had him under its control and he was a slave to its every command. Everything else was secondary. So long as he had a constant supply of drugs, his life was going exactly according to plan.

'That's smackheads for you,' Willy told me as we discussed the day's events in his cell a few hours later. 'Some of them will do anything for it. I bet some of these would take a cock for it if they thought that no one would find out.' He had a particularly unpleasant way of phrasing things. Besides, he had been smoking heroin from the moment he got up, presumably some that Johnny had smuggled onto the wing up his rectum. 'Don't get me wrong,' he added, 'I'd go through the next man's shit for drugs. That's how they get you. Especially gear – it plays tricks with your mind.' So Johnny had been fooled by his own subconscious into thinking that using the funeral as a drug-smuggling operation was the right thing to do. Heroin was a powerful and persuasive substance – one that I would never consider taking in a million years after all that I'd heard.

Johnny's actions were testament to the effect that drugs could have upon a person's mind. He had placed the need to satisfy his cravings above the need to mourn his mother's death. The other inmates saw him as deeply disrespectful and immoral, but to me he just seemed desperate. From what I had seen of him, he was not a bad person. He was just in the upper echelons of addiction. Heroin was his master and he was forever at its mercy – doomed to live a life of servitude until he gained the strength to fight.

CHAPTER 13

SMITHY

Smithy was a character who seemed far too nice to have done the things he had. He was quiet and softly spoken and rarely had a bad word to say about anyone on the wing. This was in stark contrast to his reputation on the landings. Like many criminals he was something of a social chameleon. He came across as laid back and easygoing, but, given the slightest provocation, he could easily snap. Never judge a book by its cover, because sometimes the most ruthless individuals are the ones who don't seem ruthless at all.

'I may seem like a nice guy but I've done a lot of bad things,' Smithy grinned. 'Just because I don't screw my face up on the wing, it doesn't mean that I'm not a gangster.' Several other people had said the same thing about him. If the rumours were true, he was one of the hardest people in the jail. 'What have you done, then?' I

LOWLIFE

asked. 'Let's take it from the start,' he said. 'Then you can see why I am the way I am.'

Smithy's introduction to violence had come courtesy of his father. He was beaten all the way through his childhood, whether he had done anything wrong or not. 'He was a bit of a bastard,' he told me. 'I think if it wasn't for him I wouldn't have turned out the way I did.' Violence breeds violence, and, maybe if he had been raised in a different environment, he would not have been so quick to use his fists. As it was, he was used to being hit and had no fear of confrontation.

At 13, Smithy had developed a fascination with guns. He would go out shooting birds and rabbits on the weekend and loved the sense of power he gained from holding a firearm. It came second only to the rush of adrenaline that he got from hitting people. Boxing was his way of fuelling this passion. It helped him to vent his anger and channelled his unhealthy levels of aggression into something positive. It also helped to keep him on the straight and narrow. Several of his friends were beginning to experiment with drugs, but he was unwilling to do anything that would compromise his fitness. He wanted to be a hard man and he was willing to put in the work to achieve his ambition.

At 15, he realised that there was money to be made from the vices of his peers. Although he was still drug-free himself, it was impossible to escape the fact that everyone around him was now smoking weed. It seemed like an easy way to make some quick cash. He would save up his money and buy an ounce every few weeks to sell on. The more he sold, the more people wanted. Within a few months, he was buying 50 kilos of soap bar – low-quality hash – at a time. This was at a cost of £40,000 and generated £35,000 in profit. It was a lot of money for him to be making before he had even reached adulthood.

While cannabis was the drug of choice for the local estate kids, the students in the area tended to gravitate more towards cocaine and ecstasy. The main dealers soon cottoned onto this and set about exploiting it. They knew that Smithy was doing well with his weed business and recruited him to deliver coke to the student halls, giving him a few lines out of every gram as payment for his services. He was careful to moderate his drug intake so as not to develop an addiction and undo the good work he had done at the gym.

Selling for the pre-established coke dealers served as something of an apprenticeship. Within no time at all he had learned the ropes and knew the prices and strengths of various types of cocaine. Students from all over the city soon knew him as the man to come to for drugs and he quickly developed a knack for what he did. It was time to go self-employed – he couldn't carry on being paid in coke for ever. It had been a raw deal from the start, but he had been willing to go along with it, because he had wanted to learn the trade. Now that he was fully clued up he could do it all by himself and keep 100 per cent of the profits.

Soon the coke had snowballed even more than the weed had. Smithy was now making a good £20,000 a week. He was buying a kilo at a time for £28,000 and cutting it with an equal amount of creatine (a body-building supplement) so that one kilo was effectively two. Confiscation orders had just come into existence and he was careful not to bank any of his drugs money. He would hide it all in plastic bags buried around the local area.

After a while, people began to ask Smithy if he could get hold of harder drugs for them. Because he sold coke it was often assumed he sold crack and heroin as well, so he was often approached by junkies looking for a fix. Smithy soon realised that if he was going to maximise his profits he would have to cater for all tastes. He knew a dealer in Bradford who sold wholesale amounts of heroin and bought a couple of kilos off him to sell them on. Crack could be made fairly easily by heating up a mixture of cocaine and baking soda. The next time he was asked for crack or heroin he would have it there ready to dish out.

'I was a little apprehensive at first,' Smithy told me. 'Most people who buy coke work nine-to-fives but most people who buy smack or crack are out mugging old grannies and burgling houses.' The other problem was that you couldn't cut crack or heroin as easily as coke. He could no longer rip his customers off and get away with it. On the plus side, the money was good. Crackheads and smackheads are guaranteed to come back for more. He didn't trust them, though. They were the types who would grass you up for a tenner. And, in the end, that was pretty much what had happened.

'I reckon I've got a good idea of who put my name in.' Smithy gave a resigned look, as if he knew all too well who it was but couldn't do anything about it. 'I can't prove it,' he added. His first prison sentence had been a shock to the system. 'I was scared.' This was a first – most inmates I had spoken to had acted like their first time inside was nothing. 'But then as soon as I got on the wing I saw a few people I knew and everything was kush [good].' That was one benefit of living in an area with a high crime rate. No matter what jail they put him in, he was bound to be among friends.

In the time leading up to his sentencing date, Smithy had left some drugs, guns and a large sum of money in the care of one of his friends. He didn't want the cops to come snooping round the estate while he was in jail and dig up a load of smack and firearms. His friend had no criminal record and seemed like the ideal person to look after them. Unfortunately, he was also a loudmouth. He bragged to anyone and everyone about how much money he had in his house and ended up getting burgled. A handgun, some money and some heroin were taken and he was left wondering what Smithy was going to do to him when he got out.

'*Where's the rest of it?*' Smithy bellowed. His former friend hung his head in shame. 'Someone stole it,' he mumbled back, his eyes fixed firmly upon the ground. This was not on. No one should have even known there was anything of value there to steal in the first place. An example would have to be made. There was no way that this could be allowed to happen again.

Smithy waited a few weeks until his friend had assumed that all was forgiven. He then poured petrol through his letterbox, threw a match in and ran for cover. Within seconds the whole place was ablaze. An hour later, what had once been a council house was now a smouldering pile of ash. Mission accomplished. His former friend would know to hold his tongue the next time he was given something to hold. But there wasn't going to be a next time: where there was once friendship there was now only mutual hatred.

'The next time I saw him I tried to run him over,' Smithy told me. 'I was hurt by what a bad friend he'd been. To me loyalty is everything.' In a world where loose lips could result in life sentences, it was imperative that he surround himself only with people he could trust. 'In the end, he threatened to go to the cops. I said I'd leave him alone but that we were finished as friends.' This was probably a given, anyway.

During his first time in jail, Smithy had met a new friend who he hoped would not be a letdown. They had become very close over the past few months and had agreed to do business together when they got out. His friend's family were smugglers and brought regular shipments of cocaine across from Colombia and Venezuela via Holland. His plan was to buy a kilo from him and see what his coke was like. Then, if he got good feedback from his customers, he could use him as his main supplier. He was a little wary, as he would have to travel to his house in Moss Side to do this. He had heard of the area's reputation for violence and was naturally apprehensive about venturing into one of its roughest estates with no knowledge of the area. As it turned out, he was right to be cautious.

'Get down on the bloody ground!' The minute the door was opened he had found himself staring down the barrel of a gun. There were three masked men standing in the doorway – two with knives and one with a pistol. He did exactly as he was told. 'Open your mouth!' the gunman shouted. Smithy opened his mouth and felt the cold steel nozzle of a pistol entering it. 'I want your money, the keys to your car and your trainers.' It was a set-up. His so-called friend was tied up in the corner of the room and had a few cuts and bruises on but him it was obvious that he had tipped them off. How else would they have known what day he was coming? 'Actually, keep your trainers,' laughed the main aggressor. 'I don't even want them!'

Smithy didn't care about the money – he was just pleased to have left with his life. The problem with working with other criminals was that, by their very nature, they were likely to be dishonest and try to pull a fast one at any given opportunity. He glanced over at his former companion with a look of complete disdain. 'If you want the money that badly, keep it,' he told him.

'I never wanted to see him again!' I couldn't blame him. 'Although I did have a bit of trouble over his niece a few months later!' This was mind-boggling. After he had been held up at gunpoint and robbed of a large sum of money, Smithy was still willing to associate with a member of this guy's family. 'What happened?' I asked. 'Well . . . what trouble do girls normally cause you?' he laughed. 'I was sticking it to her and her family didn't like it. The trouble wasn't from him, though – it was from her dad, this travelling fella.' Half black and half Gypsy – this was an unusual combination.

The girl's father wasn't too pleased about her seeing Smithy on account of his reputation as a prolific womaniser. He offered to have a straightener with him to settle things on the condition that, if he won, his daughter was strictly out of bounds. Smithy agreed. 'Gypsies are good fighters!' he told me. 'I should know – I've fought a few of them! A lot of my friends are travellers – they are all in on the coke game nowadays.' This was news to me – I knew that Gypsies could dabble in petty crime but had no idea that they sold drugs. 'Trust me,' Smithy smiled, 'the travellers are at the top level of every crime you can think of.'

The straightener was to be held down at the local boxing gym. The travellers were already taking bets on who would win. For them, this was a regular occurrence. Straighteners were the standard way of settling family disputes and there was one every few months. Big crowds would gather to watch and sometimes a DVD of the event would be sold afterwards.

'When you're fighting with the Gypsies there are no rules,' Smithy explained. 'Biting, eye gouging and kicking in the nads are all standard. He started off by putting his fingers in my eyes and pressing them back into my head.' Ouch. 'The crowd was split – half of it was my mates and half of it was his family. Some of them were shouting for him to blind me. I bit him on the chest and he soon let go, though.' This was real fighting – anything went, even the use of weaponry. 'I managed to throw him out of the ring and he picked up this big piece of wood and started braying me with it. In the end

I got him on the floor with his head between my legs and elbowed him hard in the back. While he was winded I kicked him in the jaw and knocked him out.'

Smithy was victorious. He could see the girl as often as he liked and there was nothing her family could do about it. 'I got bored with her after a few weeks,' he laughed. 'It was a good experience, though – I got a lot more respect off the travellers after it had all died down. I started going to watch fights with them up and down the country.'

These fights would frequently erupt into all-out warfare. They were used as a means of settling long-running disputes and often turned into mass brawls or knife fights. 'There was one fight in Darlington where the family who had lost started firing off random shots into the crowd.' I had never heard of Gypsies using guns – I knew they often carried knives but this was a new one on me. 'Are you joking?' Smithy exclaimed. 'Nowadays I'd say most of them carry guns. They've got everything from shotguns to MAC-10s.'

To keep himself safe, Smithy wore a bulletproof vest at every straightener he went to. He also took along his own firepower just in case: he would pay a smackhead to travel down in a separate car with a boot full of guns. Just in case he couldn't get to them in time, a number of baseball bats and machetes were stashed around each travelling site as backup.

Before long, Smithy had met another Gypsy girl at one of these events and started dating her. Her family had approved this time so there was no need to fight for her.

Within a few weeks, things had started getting serious. This wasn't like the last girl – it was more than just sex. He really cared about her. The only thing that was slightly offputting was her choice of friends. They were, for want of a better word, slags.

'I warned them to stay away from her but they wouldn't listen.' His brow creased as he talked and he began to look angry. 'They were a bunch of slappers. She was a good girl but if they are all going out whoring it up every weekend then she's bound to follow.' Smithy felt these girls were a bad influence and that steps would have to be taken to prevent them from leading his girlfriend astray. 'The first girl got her house torched. The second one I bought a Rottweiler, stove its head in with a lump hammer and threw the body through her window.' This was like something out of a Mafia film. 'I never saw her again after that. That's the one thing I've done that I really regretted, though – I'm a dog lover. I should have never done that to the dog.'

Violence was creeping more and more into his everyday life: it was getting to the point where anyone who slighted Smithy in any way would suffer drastic consequences. It didn't matter who they were – they would know not to do it again. His love of fighting was becoming increasingly difficult to suppress. When he was sober he was capable of calculated acts of revenge, but when he was drunk he would react instantaneously. Friday and Saturday nights were fight nights and whatever pub he happened to be in was the venue.

One night Smithy was drinking with his friends

when a drunken reveller barged into him and spilt his drink. Without saying a word, Smithy stood up and head-butted him, sending him sprawling backwards across a table. The man's two friends weren't too happy about this and immediately armed themselves with glasses and beer bottles, ready for combat. Little did they know Smithy was good friends with the bouncers and any fights that he got into would be blamed on the other person.

But the doormen arrived on the scene seconds too late. Smithy had been clubbed over the head with a bottle and glassed in the face. He had given as good as he'd got, though: the two men were covered in bruises and dripping with blood. 'Get them out!' Smithy roared. They were going to get it even worse now – the bouncers would stamp all over their heads as punishment.

Rather than going to hospital to get his wounds stitched, Smithy and his friends went on to another pub. His shirt was now a dark burgundy and he had blood pouring from a deep gash above his eye. The first thing he did was to head off to the toilets to try to get himself cleaned up. Already in a foul mood, he was getting a lot of funny looks and it was starting to irritate him.

'Some kid in the toilets was in the way of the sinks, so I gave him a smack. You know how it is when you're pissed and you're all fired up!' I nodded my head in agreement, despite the fact that I don't drink and I haven't been in a fight since I was about ten years old. 'One of my mates came in and started having a go at me. He was saying there was no need and that I'd ruined the night. Right that second, our other mate came in and smacked some next guy at the urinal for no reason!' After driving home paralytically drunk, the three of them laughed about the night's events while snorting coke to keep them awake. To them it was all a big joke.

Smithy had always aspired to be physically intimidating. From his early childhood it had been his dream to be a boxer. Now that he was handy with his fists, he felt it a shame to restrict them to the ring. Whether straighteners or bar brawls, he relished every opportunity to prove himself. Maybe it was the beatings he had received as a child that had made him like this. Maybe he had violence in his genes. Whatever the reason, he was a dangerous man. The fact that he was able to disguise his temperament made it even more of a threat. His victims had no idea what lay in store for them until it was too late. The respect he had gained from the Gypsies was testament to his skills as a fighter. These people had been trained to box from prepubescence. His fists were dangerous weapons and were brandished far too readily.

'Violence is all I've really known,' he said. 'It's the only thing I can rely on.' This was true – it was the basis of his chosen career and the cement that held together his turbulent existence. He knew no other way of gaining respect. In his world, might equalled right and the only way of ensuring loyalty was through punishing those who were disloyal. His fists were weapons but they were also the tools of his trade. They were his livelihood. Without them he would be out of a job.

CHAPTER 14
BIG CHRIS

Smithy's revelations about travellers drastically altered the way in which I perceived them. As with most marginalised people, there were a disproportionate number of them in the prison, but I had always seen them as more likely to be street brawlers or pub fighters than drug dealers or gunrunners. They were always highly respected on the wing, but I had assumed that this was because of their aptitude for fist fighting rather than the severity of their crimes. Some inmates even trailed upon their coat tails and attempted to be Gypsy-by-association. They affected their dialect and mannerisms and even spoke of moving in with them in their caravans once they had been released. This was a measure of the level of admiration that they received from the other inmates. To some, they were definite role models.

Romani words such as 'shiv' (a knife) and 'chor' (to

steal) were used by Gypsies and non-Gypsies alike throughout the jail. 'There's a lot of Gypsy words that people just think of as prison slang,' one traveller explained to me. 'Things like "radge" [mad], "mush" [man], "bewer" [a woman] and "kushty" [good] – they are all Romani. "Gadge" as well – people in here use it like "mate" but it actually means a non-Gypsy.' The influence of the travellers on the jail population was undeniable. Gypsy culture and prison culture were very much intertwined.

My preconceived image of a Gypsy was one of a haggard old man with an Irish or Eastern European accent. This couldn't have been further from the truth. Most of the travellers on the wing were indistinguishable from the rest of the prison population. Many of them were second- or third-generation Gypsies and had been brought up in council houses as opposed to caravans. They were still involved in traditional Gypsy pastimes such as boxing and horse riding but for the most part, they were just like everyone else. One of the few Gypsies on the wing who had carried on living the traditional travelling way of life was a guy called Big Chris, who spoke in an English accent heavily peppered with Romani slang. He referred to me as 'Simon mush' and anything he approved of came under the category of 'kush' – a shortened version of 'kushty'.

'I grew up in a caravan eating hedgehog,' he told me. Was he joking? 'Nah, it's a Gypsy delicacy – it tastes a bit like chicken mixed with veal. We used to cook 'em in a ground oven. Bloody gorgeous they were. I don't think you're allowed to eat them nowadays, though – aren't they an endangered species or something?' I couldn't help but wonder what had possessed him to eat hedgehog. 'That's the Gypsy way,' he explained. 'We live off the land. We don't claim any benefits, so money is usually scarce and we have to eat what we can get.'

This was just one of many problems facing the travelling community. A good number of them were illiterate and uneducated and found it hard to get work, but, as they had no fixed address, they also found it difficult to claim any of the benefits to which they were entitled. The only path left for them was that of the grafter. 'The rest of my family would never have done anything illegal,' he carried on, giving the impression that he now had to say something in defence of his people to balance out any negative opinion that I might have formed. 'My parents were law-abiding citizens. They came over from Palermo during the war and settled in the Lake District.' Palermo is a Sicilian city infamous for organised crime and corruption. His family had wanted to bring him up in a less crime-driven environment, but the Cumbrian Gypsy population harboured more than its fair share of crooks and villains.

Chris was from a tough family – his father was a notorious bare-knuckle boxer and his mother had seen her fair share of hardship, as had most Gypsy women. Despite this, they lived a peaceful existence and chose a life of subsistence over one that was reliant upon crime. It was not until he was in his early twenties that Chris even considered crime as an option. There were a number of older travellers on the site who seemed to have a never-ending supply of wealth. They were covered in expensive gold jewellery and never seemed to go short of anything. What was their secret? he wondered.

There was no real secret about how they earned their money: they were car thieves. Although he had smoked a bit of weed and done a few Es in his teens, Chris was fairly strait-laced. This made him all the more eager to experience the other side of life. 'The Romani word for money is "love",' he told me. 'It's no coincidence either. I wanted the things I could never afford and here was an easy way of getting them.' At first he had started stealing cars just to see what it felt like. Soon he had developed a taste for it and became addicted to the buzz.

The site Chris was living on was in a small mining village called Parton. Every weekend he would get drunk and drive stolen cars at high speed along the main road. It was only a matter of time before the police caught up with him. They were suspicious of the Gypsies as it was, and would come to the site asking questions whenever anything went missing, regardless of whether they had taken it or not. Although it had become fairly deprived after the closure of its coalmines, Parton still had a relatively low level of car crime. The sudden increase in stolen vehicles shortly after the travellers arrived had meant that they were watched very closely indeed. Within a few months, Chris had been caught red-handed in the front seat of a TWOC.

Chris enjoyed his first time in a young offenders'. He found it exciting. 'It was the first place where I met people who were as wild as me,' he smiled. 'I was getting into fights as often as I could and I loved a good scrap back then. That place was like a university – I learned so much about crime there it was unreal.' Chris knew exactly what he was going to do when he got out – turn his hobby into a full-time job. He was too old for joyriding, anyway. It was time for him to start earning a living – and then some.

The Appleby Horse Fair is a good place to meet fences. An annual horse show, it attracts 10,000 travellers from all over Europe – many of them law-abiding citizens but a sizeable minority involved in buying and selling stolen goods. The fair has been subject to significant controversy and marred by a number of violent incidents over the years. The past few events have seen a stabbing, a mass brawl and countless arrests for drugs and illegal weapons. The majority of attendees are happy to ride their horses along the river in peace but, as is to be expected from any gathering of poor, oppressed people, there is always a small contingent of troublemakers.

These troublemakers were the people Chris had come to see. They were the ones who could give him orders for cars to steal. Stealing to order was more profitable than taking cars at random and always guaranteed him a buyer. There was a thriving market for caravans as well. They were exported all over Europe through a criminal network of travellers. 'You could put nitric acid in the locks and burn the tumblers out,' he told me. For someone who had never been charged with caravan theft, he sure knew a lot about it. 'One way of doing it was to go to a storage yard, put a shitty old caravan in so you got a pair of keys to the place, and then come back and take all the good ones. They were normally worth around £20,000 each but they would get sold on for £4,000 odd.'

It didn't stop there. Chris had 'friends' who would steal anything that wasn't nailed down. 'You could make a packet from hot-dog stands. They were worth about 20 grand new! Horse boxes were another one.' As time went on, the methods used in these thefts got more and more elaborate. One way of robbing commercial premises was to go in as a customer during the day, spray the alarm sensors with carpet glue and put expandable foam in the alarm boxes while the staff weren't looking. This meant the thief could sneak in undetected that night and help themselves to whatever they wanted.

'It was a lot easier back in the day – they had less security than they do nowadays.' I had heard this from several of the middle-aged burglars. 'You could start a car with a penknife or even a spoon if you knew what you were doing. The doors could be prised open with a slide hammer. It was easy pickings.' He was working nine to five and the more cars he stole, the better he became at it.

Now he had a regular income, there would be no more foraging for hedgehogs. Chris could eat like a king. He carried on living in a caravan in deference to his roots but could have afforded a stately home had he wanted one. He was also kitted out in all the latest football-terrace fashions. Casual wear was all the rage among his criminal associates and everything he wore was Rockport, Hugo Boss, Fila or Sergio Tacchini.

The best time to show off his designer clobber was on a match day. He used to hang around with nearby Carlisle United's hooligans, known as the Border City Firm, and they would compete to see who was the best dressed. 'The terraces were like a fashion parade in those days,' he laughed. 'There was a way of life that went with the clothing, though, and I ended up getting caught up in the fighting as well.'

The first time Chris had encountered football violence he was at an away game in Blackpool. He was standing with a crew of around 300 Border City Firm when 50 members of Blackpool's Seaside Mafia firm charged over ready for combat. But the BCF were armed with an assortment of weaponry, including iron bars and telescopic truncheons, and absolutely pulverised them. They outmanned them and left them strewn bloody and semiconscious across the concrete. Chris was in the thick of it and loved every minute. From that moment onwards, he attended every clash the BCF were involved in and lived for hooliganism.

'I normally had a blade on me. Sometimes it was just a Stanley but others I'd have a flick knife or a stiletto. They could slice a mush up proper.' It was lucky he'd never killed anyone. 'If there was a lot of coppers about, we'd take fountain pens. If you stabbed someone with one of them you could do a lot of damage, but they couldn't do you for them if they found them on you.' It didn't stop there, though. 'We used to tape blades onto 2p coins and throw them like darts. The worst damage I ever did was with my fists, though. I belted this guy in the throat in Exeter and thought I'd killed him, but in the end he came round and was OK – he just had the wind knocked out of him.'

At that time the BCF's main rival was Millwall's Bushwackers firm – bizarre, seeing that they were based at opposite ends of the country. Millwall FC are more famous for their hooligans than their actual team. 'I have to admit they've quite a naughty little firm,' Chris conceded. 'Their speciality was the Millwall brick. They'd get a newspaper, roll it up really tightly and then attach a shoelace to one end. They'd swing it at you and it was like being hit with a mace! You wouldn't have believed a rolled-up newspaper could hurt that much. Sometimes they put a nail through it as well just to make it extra-lethal.' Hooligans could be remarkably resourceful. Another commonly used weapon was a knuckleduster made out of pennies held together with strips of paper. The police could hardly confiscate all the loose change that the fans had in their pockets, so there was no way of preventing them from making them.

When car theft is your full-time job and hooliganism is your favourite pastime it is difficult to keep a clean slate. Chris had served more sentences than he cared to remember. It was a given if you lived a life of crime that you would get put away every now and again, but this didn't mean that he had to stop earning during this period. 'There was this "friend" I had,' he smiled. 'He was shagging this screw and getting her to bring in all sorts for him.' This wasn't uncommon: I had heard stories from several different inmates about staff sleeping with prisoners, and some female officers seemed to have an infatuation with certain inmates in their charge. It was almost as if they got off on how dangerous they were. There was even talk of nurses in a certain high-security jail charging inmates for sex.

Chris's 'friend' was getting a female prison guard to bring in phones and drugs for him. 'There was this one screwess [female prison officer] who proper took a shine to him,' he told me. 'She would have done anything for him. One day when he came back from the gym she was being all flirty and saying, "Oh, you look all sweaty there!" He told her, "I'll show you sweat!"' This screwess became overfamiliar with Chris over the following weeks. She had sat in his cell and talked to him for hours on end. The word was that he'd been sleeping with her and that he had her firmly under the thumb.

'She had a secret phrase she used when she wanted it so that the other kangas [prison guards] wouldn't know what was going on. When she was up for it she'd say, "Can you help me mop up this water?" Then they'd both go into the cleaning cupboard and he'd give her a good seeing-to. I believe the first time he did her, he back-scuttled her and it was all over in about five seconds.' Chris's 'friend' hadn't been the only one she had slept with. 'One day this other travelling fella wanted a go too so my "friend" fed her this big sob story. He told her that it was this mush's birthday and he was really depressed 'cause his aunt had just died. She went with him and all! Her head had gone a bit by then, though – she was taking far too much coke.'

This jailhouse romance continued for a good few months and proved highly profitable. The screwess would meet an outside contact every two weeks in Carlisle McDonald's and have a bag full of cocaine and cannabis passed over to her in a Happy Meal bag. This would be smuggled into the prison and sold on for five times its street value. She was also bringing in mobile phones. She flooded the jail with more than 400 of them, despite the fact that the overall population of the prison was only 1,000, and sneaked in vodka disguised in plastic Evian bottles. 'The funniest thing was that her husband was a copper! They started calling my "friend" Nokia because he was selling so many phones in there.'

Eventually, Chris was transferred to an open jail and left 'Nokia' and the love-blind screw behind. Now that he was in a less secure category of prison, he was allowed visits to the local town at weekends, although this was not as much of a benefit as you might have thought. It was like dangling a piece of bait in front of a hungry carp. He had to be back within a certain timescale and he was expected to return of his own volition at the end of each visit. Eventually the temptation proved too much for him. The good thing about being a traveller was that he had no fixed abode – he was almost impossible for the authorities to locate. One day, instead of going back to the prison, he got a pal to pick him up and went to stay with some of his travelling friends in Cannock near Stafford. He was now a prison escapee.

Chris was on the run for nine months before he finally gave himself up. The police repeatedly raided his mum's caravan looking for him until she rang him up begging him to surrender himself. Not wanting to cause her any further hassle, he went to the nearest police station and handed himself in. Nearly every prisoner I met who had been in an open prison had absconded from it. This resulted in their being transferred to closed conditions and having a few months added to their sentence. This was effectively a slap on the wrist and did very little to deter future absconders.

'It gave me a break from prison life – I got to do my own thing for a few months and had no restrictions. At the end of the day, an extra month odd is nothing.' In the scheme of things, it was a blink of the eye, considering that some people in open prisons were coming towards the end of life sentences. 'Within no time I was out doing pretty much the same things as I'd been doing before.'

Family are very important to the Romani people and Chris felt ashamed of what he had put his mum through. 'Look at my son, though,' he said. 'He didn't exactly turn out how I expected him to. He's a poof! He came into the trailer one day wearing a wig and makeup and said, "Dad, this is who I am!" He was only 13!' I was curious as to how he had reacted to this. Many prisoners were very vocal in their opposition to homosexuality, as if condemning those who were gay or bisexual somehow reinforced their own heterosexual status. 'I was devastated!' he replied, predictably. 'I took him down to a knocking shop and thought that I could get him to snap out of it by getting him a whore. He cried his eyes out, so in the end I had to accept him for who he was.' At least he had done the right thing in the end, even though it was highly irresponsible taking such a young boy to a brothel. 'I've got nothing against poofs,' he clarified. 'I just never thought I'd end up with one as a son!'

'Does he do any type of crime, then?' I inquired, interested to see if Chris had passed on his trade to the next generation. 'Nah – he's far too gay for all of that!' he chortled. 'He must be the only gay traveller I've ever met! Look at him in this picture!' He held up a photo of a tracksuited youth playing with a dog. 'Look at the dog! He's got a poodle – a poof's dog!' For all he poked fun at his son's sexuality, it was affectionate rather than malicious and it was obvious that he still had a father's love for him.

Being a gay Romani must be tough. It is hard enough being a Romani in the first place. They have the highest rates of illiteracy and infant mortality of all Britain's minority groups and suffer from a range of social problems, including poverty, discrimination and lack of access to education and healthcare. Small wonder they often feel the need to resort to crime! One of the other main issues affecting the travelling community is that of substance abuse. As with many poor minority groups, crack and heroin addiction have taken their toll. Chris had had first-hand experience of this. He had been to hell and back. And then back to hell again.

He had first encountered heroin partway through his current sentence. He had been bored one day and decided to have a go on a smack pipe to see what all the fuss was about. It was better than he had expected – far more pleasurable than any other drug he had tried, and he had done his fair share of experimenting. He couldn't wait to do it again.

Within a few months, Chris was spending all his money on smack and getting himself increasingly into debt. He looked permanently wired and his friends were beginning to notice the change in him. Whereas he had once been friendly and sociable, he now spent large periods of time alone in his cell with a piece of foil and a solid brown lump of heroin for company. It was his escape from reality. When he was smoking smack he felt as if he were free from all his worries and responsibilities and could sit and while away the time without a care in the world. This was a delusion. He owed money to some very dangerous people and, if he didn't pay them soon, he would be in big trouble.

After months of self-denial, Chris finally began to admit to himself that he had a problem. 'How's it going?' I asked him one day as we queued up for our meal, just as a conversation starter. He looked worried. 'I've got a raging smack addiction! I think I'm going to book myself in with CARAT.' CARAT stands for Counselling, Assessment, Referral, Advice and Throughcare. It is the prison's drug rehabilitation service. This was his first step to recovery. He was actively seeking help.

Chris was given Subutex to help wean himself off heroin. It worked insofar as it got him off the smack, but the downside was that he was now hooked on Subutex. Rather than take the tablets orally as advised, he crushed them up and snorted them, since this provided him with a greater buzz. He still owed money for the smack he had bought, so the fact that he was now buying Subutex on the black market put him on a slippery slope.

'Where's my money, you fat smackhead?' one of the dealers eventually bellowed in his face, looking very close to beating him to a bloody pulp. Chris looked scared. He was no stranger to a fistfight, but in jail it was different. People wouldn't stop when you were on the floor – they would kick you even harder. They were also the types who would come back the next day and stab you. He was going to have to do something to get himself out of this situation or he might not survive until the end of his sentence.

'That filthy debt-head's blocked himself off!' Well, it was either that or get a kicking. He had asked the guards to place him down the segregation unit for his own protection and effectively got himself out of paying off his debt. He owed a few hundred pounds, which is a lot of money in prison. The dealers on the wing were raging. 'If I ever see him again I'm going to stab his eyes out,' the main heroin dealer snarled. The news soon reached the unit that Chris would be getting transferred to another prison. Had he stayed, he would have been a wanted man.

That was the last I ever saw of possibly Britain's only smack-addicted Gypsy football hooligan. He was certainly one of a kind. No matter how much money he earned through crime, he always stayed true to his Gypsy roots and lived in a caravan. However, it was men like him who perpetuated the stereotype of Gypsies as thieves and villains, and I couldn't help feeling that it was people like him who were holding the Romanies back.

Drugs are taboo among the Romani population and are seen as the domain of the sinful 'gadges' (non-Gypsies). Whereas some interpretations of Gypsy law sanction certain acts of petty crime, violence is viewed as abhorrent to the Romani way of life. The way in which Chris lived his life was betraying his culture and turning his back on the traditions of the travelling community. He may have lived in a caravan, but this was as far as his allegiance to the Romanies went. Until he changed his ways, he could never class himself as a true Gypsy.

CHAPTER 15
CODY

Perhaps one of the few groups in society on a par with the Romanies in terms of deprivation and lack of education are the Irish travellers. Only two-thirds of the population survive past the age of 25 and only a fifth reach 65. They have survival rates akin to those of a Third World country. The vast majority have no formal qualifications and their levels of literacy and numeracy are well below the national average. Coupled with the discrimination they face on a daily basis, these factors guarantee that plenty of them will be involved in crime.

Cody was one such traveller. He had grown up in Belfast and his upbringing had been far from stable. He was raised around guns and drugs, and his father had been in and out of prison. On top of this, his family were constantly having wars with rival travelling clans, which would often result in bloodshed. 'Sometimes it was just fists,' he told me. 'A lot of the time it was blades as well

LOWLIFE

and sometimes they used guns. There were a lot of guns on the site I was staying at – people there were selling them to the IRA [Irish Republican Army] and the UVF [Ulster Volunteer Force]. They were all backing the IRA but didn't really care who they sold them to – all they cared about was the money.'

I was curious to see where Cody's allegiance lay. 'Up the IRA!' he grinned. 'Ireland wouldn't be what it is today without them. I don't agree with everything that they've done but I agree a hundred per cent with what they stand for.' So why would a member of the UVF buy guns from a group of IRA supporters? 'They wouldn't tell them who they were backing,' Cody explained. 'Plus, the travellers go abroad a lot, so they're in a good position to bring things back with them.'

What with the paramilitary presence and relative poverty of certain areas in the city, Belfast had a major problem with guns. 'Everyone had a piece back then – it was crazy!' Cody told me. 'My old man got locked up for guns. We had ourselves a feud with another travelling family and the police claimed he'd tried to kill one of them. They raided our caravan and found two double-barrel shotguns. He got done for firearms and attempted murder and went away for a long one.'

Despite having grown up around so much crime, by the age of 14 Cody had decided that he was going to try to eke out an honest living. He started off tarmacking drives and then went on to laying PVC guttering. He was earning just enough to get by and it was often difficult to find work. While he was struggling to earn a legal crust, a constant stream of smackheads were coming onto the travellers' site to sell stolen power tools. The travellers had a reputation for being good fences, and addicts would come from far and wide to see what they could offload on them. After a few months of working his back out for peanuts, Cody finally caved in and bought some tools to sell. He had tried to go straight. It simply hadn't paid enough.

Cody had done OK from selling the tools, but he longed for more cash. 'The thing about us travelling folk is we have a love of money,' he told me. 'It's been like that for centuries. That's why a lot of us turn to crime.' He had heard of other travellers in the area stealing caravans from England and exporting them to the Republic of Ireland to sell to the fences there. 'That's where the real money was. People were bringing them back on the ferry and selling them for £4,000 each. I probably would have done around two a week if I'd have done that.'

Cody's first conviction was at age 19 for wounding with intent. He had slashed a man with a Stanley knife during a drunken bar fight. 'He pulled his knife out and tried to threaten me with it, so I whipped mine out and cut his face with it.' The way he described it was as if this were nothing. He got four and a half years and took to life in a young offenders' institution like a fish to water. 'I walked onto the wing and saw a load of me old pals,' he told me. 'It was like being back on the site again!'

Jail did nothing to rehabilitate Cody, and the minute he got out he was up to his old tricks again. 'All it did was make me try even harder not to get caught!' he laughed. 'The hardest crime for the coppers to get you for was selling rung cars. If you got caught, you could just say that you didn't know that they were stolen. I knew this guy – he looked a bit like me: similar height and build, same appearance – travelling fella from Belfast. He was getting £500 a week from it.'

Fraud was another crime the travellers specialised in. 'The fellas would tarmac people's drives and then demand twice as much money as they had asked for once the job was done. If they didn't pay up they'd get their driveway smashed up with a pickaxe and sometimes they'd get threatened too.' Had Cody stuck to the rung vans and the frauds then he might have stayed out of jail. As it was, he couldn't resist the money that was to be had from stealing caravans. This soon came to the attention of the police, who received information that he was involved in a break-in at a garage in Leicester and put a warrant out for his arrest. He was able to avoid apprehension for quite some time until he was eventually stopped by Holyhead police with a stolen caravan in tow. He was given a total of three years inside.

'It's a long one for what it is, this one!' he sighed. 'I think I've done enough jail now – I'm going to go back to the guttering when I get out. The pay's not great but at least it keeps you out of this place! Now where's that quarter of burn you said you'd give me for telling you all of this?' I gave a wry smile. I hadn't offered him anything of the sort, but it was easier to go along with him. The

Gypsies had a lot of clout on the wing and it was important to keep them on side. 'I'll put it down for you on this week's shop order,' I told him.

'Why do you think that there are so many travellers involved in crime, then?' I asked. 'Do you think it's because of the discrimination against them?' He looked puzzled. 'No one's ever discriminated against me,' he replied. The likelihood was that any prejudice that people might have harboured would have been kept to themselves, as he did not seem the type of person who would have taken kindly to it. 'No, it's because we love money. Travellers are greedy!' he chortled. 'I'll be the first to admit it!' But what had this stemmed from? It would be easy to pass his materialism off as mere greed but it was most probably the result of growing up poor and wanting the things that he had never been able to have.

'How long have you got left to go?' I asked, attempting to round the conversation off, as I felt I might owe him more tobacco if it went on any longer. 'Well, it depends. I've got another charge hanging over me. This kid in the last jail I was in is saying I bust his head in with a coffee jar.' I was tempted to ask him if he had done it but I felt I already knew the answer to that one. 'He must have waited until he'd got out before grassing on me.' This would be his second wounding-with-intent charge and could land him with a long sentence. He could be in for some time.

Cody was a product of his environment and his upbringing. When a group of people are pushed towards the margins of society they are often forced to commit crime in order to survive. It is thought that up to 10 per cent of the prison population are travellers compared with 0.15 per cent of the general population. Criminality exists within their culture as a way of providing for themselves when there is little other means to do so. More and more travellers are now living in council houses and claiming benefits. This solves the problem of how to survive when there is no work available but brings with it a new set of problems. Many claim that houses are like prisons and yearn for the freedom of the travelling lifestyle. There is no simple solution to the travellers' plight. They have existed on the fringes of society for centuries and look set to do so well into the future.

CHAPTER 16

BULL'S BALLS

Scousers were another group heavily overrepresented in the prison system. Liverpool is the country's poorest local authority and contains four of the ten most deprived wards in England. It is often stereotypically associated with crime, although this is most probably as a result of the widespread poverty there. However, there are certainly areas of the city where the law of the land is definitely secondary to the law of the street.

Bull's Balls was as Scouse as they came. He spoke with a thick Liverpudlian accent and did nothing to dispel his city's negative reputation. 'Most of the top smugglers nowadays come from round our way,' he told me. 'We get our drugs straight off the boat – we're at the top of the food chain. We do it in style, too. You should get some stories off me for your book. That'd shift you a few copies!' I was curious as to what type of stories he had to tell me. 'Ones with a bit of swashbuckle to them!' he replied. 'Smugglers' stories!'

Liverpool has a long history of smuggling dating back to the 1700s, when high duties on spirits, tea and tobacco meant that local sailors would often bring such goods in illegally. Nowadays the main cargo for illegal imports into the UK is drugs. 'They've got coast patrols and all types of things but we still get 'em across. We're like modern day pirates!' He was getting excited. It seemed like he had been waiting for a willing audience to share his maritime adventures with for quite some time. 'You're looking at Liverpool's answer to Long John Silver right here!' he crowed.

Bull's Balls had brought across two main products – cocaine and cannabis. 'My family are all smugglers,' he explained. 'It's kinda like a family business. Whenever I need a bit of extra cash they ring me up and say, " 'Ere kidda, I've got a job for ya!" ' He had grown up poor on one of the city's most deprived council estates and was always glad of any extra money he could get. 'I did it for the buzz as well as the cash, though!' he elaborated. 'You get a mad rush from it, lad!'

'Why are you called Bull's Balls?' I asked. It was the question I had wanted to ask from the minute I had first heard about it. 'Well . . .' I could see him gearing up for a lengthy explanation. 'It all started with a phone call. Our Barry rings me up one day and says there's 350 kilos of weed needs taking over from the Rif mountains in Morocco. He wanted to know if I was up for bringing it across.' The Rif mountains are world's largest production area for hashish. There are several thousand hectares of *Cannabis sativa* growing there, tended to by the local farmers. The marijuana crop provides the livelihoods of some 800,000 people within the region, despite the fact that its cultivation is illegal in Morocco and is punishable by a lengthy jail sentence. 'I hopped on the plane the next day and was bang on it!'

You had to admire his enthusiasm. 'First of all, I lived up there for a couple of months and helped to press the weed into blocks. It's a mad place – there's big fields of ganja growing as far as the eye can see. The Moroccans are good people – we had a laugh with 'em! We gave 'em a few little gifts – just to get on the right side of 'em!' The mountains could get very cold at night, so Bull's Balls had decided to go prepared. He had a friend in one of Liverpool's local jails who had been hoarding prison jumpers in his cell and asked him if he would mind throwing a few over the walls to him. This must have been one of the few times when anything was ever thrown over the walls in an outward direction. He managed to chuck 20 jumpers over, all emblazoned with the prison logo. 'We handed them out to the locals and they loved 'em!' he laughed. 'Imagine that – all them Arabs parading round in HMP tops up this big mountain surrounded by weed plants!'

After a few weeks of helping out on the farms, it was time to take the weed across to Spain. 'There was a few locals who wanted to hitch a ride over, so we thought it'd be a laugh to take 'em with us! We ended up with these two Arabs who could hardly speak a word of

English sharing the boat with us!' Bull's Balls and his two newly acquired hitchhikers drove down to the coastal city of Tangiers, where their transport awaited them. This was in the form of a 12ft motorboat. 'There were two ways of getting across,' he told me. 'Sometimes we went on this boat called a Zodiac, which was fast enough to go straight across without the coppers getting on to us. The rest of the time we had to sneak around them and go a slightly longer route in a motorboat.'

The journey took a full nine hours and was by no means an easy one. Twelve-foot waves crashed all around the tiny vessel as it sped across the seas. The skies were filled with thunder and lightning and the two Moroccans spent the whole time praying for their lives. 'They kept saying for me to throw some of the packages over 'cause they were going to sink the boat. I said, "No way, lad – if anything goes over it'll be you!" ' Each package contained 25 kilos of weed with a street value of £47,500. Little wonder he had wanted to hang onto them so badly!

Bull's Balls stood boldly at the front of the boat yelling orders to his two-man crew. He was in his element. 'I was like Captain Ahab!' he told me. 'It was like that book *Moby Dick*! At one point we went across the bow of a hulking great tramp ship. They were foghorning us and looking over the side wondering what we were doing. I was just standing there loving every minute of it!'

Just as he was finally approaching the shore, disaster

struck. A huge wave hit the boat and the Moroccans flew head first into the water. Neither of them could swim, so he had to act fast to save them. He stripped down to his boxers and dived head first into the ice-cold sea to fish them out. They were only a few yards from the shore and it would have been a shame to lose them at this stage. After a brief battle with the elements, he managed to haul them both ashore and swam back to see if his cargo had survived. It was all there. He threw the bundles across to the shore, hopped out onto dry land and danced with joy.

'The Arabs were hugging me and kissing me. It was a bit over the top really! They kept telling me I had the balls of a bull! And that's how I got the name – it just stuck from there.' From that moment onwards, he was known as the man who had protected his wares at any cost. Whether this was as a result of greed, determination or sheer insanity was neither here nor there.

Bull's Balls (as he was now officially known) drove his cargo along the coast, past Estepona and into Gibraltar, where he got stuck behind a police car. He remained calm, kept his composure and carried on going – after all, he did have the balls of a bull. The police touched their brakes to see if he slowed down – a test to see if he was still fully awake, as it was now 5.30am. He immediately reduced his speed and the cop car pulled off down a side street. He had passed their test.

Eventually, he came to Marbella – a popular tourist destination on the Costa del Sol. Here he was met by two of his friends from London, who vacuum-packed the weed for him to make it easier to transport. Now that it was in Europe, it would be easy enough to smuggle it back to Liverpool. There were several different ways to do this. One of his friends owned a legitimate export company and could be paid to take a few extra parcels across every now and again. Bull's Balls also had an ingenious way of disguising drugs packages as golf clubs. One of his friends from Halewood in Liverpool was a professional thief who was known for stealing sporting equipment. Whenever he robbed a golf shop, he would pass a few of the clubs on to Bull's Balls, who would take the tops off the clubs and glue them to a sports bag so they looked as if they were sticking out of the top. Underneath would be a dense layer of whatever drug he was transporting at the time. To the untrained eye, it would look as if the bag had clubs in it and nothing else. 'The key was the fact that they were top-make club heads,' he explained. 'If it was some cheap and nasty ones they might have clocked on, but, as it was, nobody batted an eyelid.'

Whenever he returned to Liverpool after a successful smuggling operation, Bull's Balls would receive a hero's welcome. All his friends would be waiting for him and they would go out drinking and sniffing coke to celebrate. This would spur him on to go back a few months later and do the same thing again. His tales of adventure on the high seas also captured the imagination of several of his friends and he was not without his imitators. A man known as Donx, who drank at the same pub, tried to follow in his footsteps. Unfortunately, he drowned in the attempt.

'It could have been me!' Bull's Balls' voice had a tone of sadness but also a slight hint of pride. He was clearly sad at the death of his friend but at the same time revelling in the fact that he had succeeded where others had died trying. 'There was a few tried it and came a cropper. A couple of my mates went across and ended up getting in a shootout with the Moroccan busies [police]. They ended up in jail there and had an awful time. One of them got bailed out and left his mate in there. He ended up getting gang-raped and hung himself.' Moroccan prisons are infamous for sexual abuse, overcrowding, poor hygiene and violence. To risk ending up in one of those places was like risking Hell itself.

But Bull's Balls got only a fraction of the overall earnings from each trip. He got paid £20,000 for smuggling £665,000 of weed. It cost £100 a kilo and was sold for around £1,900 a kilo – his boss was making a profit of £610,000 per journey and doing none of the work himself. 'The pay could have been better!' It was a bit of a raw deal, but he was still earning at least £1,000 a week, depending on the length of the trip. 'There's no rush like it, though,' he went on. 'It's better than the best coke you can buy.' I got the feeling that Bull's Balls was something of an adrenaline junkie. He was a compulsive risk taker, addicted to danger. 'Sometimes I was the one pulling the strings, though.' He gave a disgruntled look, as if to say he would rather have been the one moving the drugs than telling other people what to do. 'People would ring me up when their smugglers had made a mess of things and get me to sort it for them.' This was testament to his expertise at what he did.

'This one time I got a call from a good mate of mine. He says there's this couple he's paid to bring a shipment of "material" across and it's gone pear-shaped.' 'Material' was what he called weed over the phone just in case his call was being tapped. 'They'd been drinking and smoking and they were having a bit of a domestic. They were shouting their heads off – what if the busies came round about the noise? They'd all be getting promotions!' An hour later, he was on a plane to Spain. This was no job for amateurs – there were hundreds of thousands of pounds at stake and these two fools were running the risk of losing them.

Bull's Balls knocked on the door to the villa where the quarrelling couple were staying. It opened. They were still bellowing at each other and their eyes were an unhealthy shade of crimson. 'Eh, you two soft shites,' he said. 'What do you think you're doing??'

'I let them know that I wasn't pleased,' he told me. Usually this would be a euphemism for hitting them with hammers or burning their house down but here he was speaking literally. 'There's no need to be getting on people's bad sides. That's when they start throwing your name around down at the cop shop. I said they'd still get their money, but I wanted them out of there right now, and if they told anyone where the weed was my family would find them and do them in.' They left straightaway and from that moment onwards, Bull's Balls was in charge of the 'material'. It got there on the dot and in mint condition, and, from then on, whenever anything needed smuggling he was always given first refusal.

'There's a lot of Scousers over in Spain,' Bull's Balls explained. 'A lot of them are moving drugs. But not a lot that are anywhere near to being in the same league as me.' Why were there so many Liverpudlians involved in the drugs trade over there? 'Well, they can't claim benefits over there, you see,' he told me. 'They work in the bars during the holiday season but the rest of the time they're out of a job, so they do grafts. A few of them get delivery jobs so they can drop packages off along the way. One of my mates used to work for a soft-drinks company. He delivered bottles to all the main resorts along the Costa del Sol, and while he was there he dropped parcels off to the main dealers there.'

The Costa del Sol has been dubbed the Costa del Crime by the tabloids and is a well-known haunt for competing drug gangs from Liverpool, London, Ireland and Eastern Europe. It has been the site of several violent incidents, including the gangland shooting of suspected Scouse drugs trafficker Marvin Herbert in 2008. 'There's always plenty needs doing there,' Bull's Balls told me. 'It gets a bit hectic at times but mostly everyone just gets on with things. They used to ferry the drugs about during the siesta, when it was quiet, but the busies are well onto it now, so it's a bit harder.'

If he was bringing cocaine across, the police were a lot less of a problem if he had money on him. Cocaine is produced by extracting a chemical from the coca plant, which is native to the northwest of South America. Colombia is home to the largest plantation of coca plants in the world and is also conveniently a hotbed of institutional corruption. For a small fee, the police were willing to look the other way and let people do whatever they wanted. This was the perfect place for Bull's Balls to do business.

'We'd go over to Bogotá, the capital city there,' he told me. 'There'd be a contact waiting who would hand the charlie over. If the coppers there pulled you, you'd have to give them the equivalent of £100 each. If there was ten of them you had to shell out a grand!' Colombian jails are some of the worst in the world, and, realistically, the police could have asked for as much as they liked and he would have had no choice but to have paid it.

The police were only a minor threat compared with various other organisations that operated in the city. Bogotá has a reputation as one of the most violent cities in the world and organised crime is rife there. A pale-faced gringo walking around with a suitcase full of bribe money was very risky indeed. It was like walking around with a big placard saying 'Rob me'. 'I was always alright, though, 'cause I had the right connections. The people I came to see weren't going to let one of their best customers get had off.' He must have known some powerful people.

Bull's Balls certainly did have the balls of a bull. He was willing to risk life and limb to feed his addiction to thrill-seeking and he clearly saw himself as something of a modern-day buccaneer. He took great pride in what he did and saw his skills as a smuggler as testament to his resourcefulness and quick-wittedness. He was one of the few inmates who didn't seem overly materialistic – the main reason he did crime was to fulfil his need for adventure.

'It's not as if I'm bringing smack across here.' This was his way of justifying what he did. He neglected the fact that cocaine could easily be cooked up into crack – an equally harmful and addictive substance. Still, he was never one to let morality get in the way of an adventure. He would merely shift his moral code to fit in with what he wanted to do.

On the day of my release, Bull's Balls came across to me on the yard and shook my hand. 'Is right, lad – hope you remember to put the modern day Long John Silver in yer book – sell you a million copies, that will!' I had a feeling that he had enjoyed telling me his story and that the next person to share a cell with him would have smuggling stories coming out of their ears. He had certainly been a character. The chances of his ever giving up smuggling were next to zero – his eyes lit up at the very mention of the word. As we said our farewells, I couldn't help thinking that he would be in the papers in a few years' time under the headline 'UK's biggest ever drugs bust'.

Bull's Balls was a crook like any other, but one who had a certain charm in the way he related his tales. He managed to talk up drug smuggling in such a way that it almost seemed like an act of heroism instead something highly illegal the world over. He was a storyteller. Everything he did, he lived to tell – whether it was good or bad. He was a master of spin – converting organised crime into adventures on the high seas. But, romanticised as they might have become, the pirates of old were nothing more than common criminals, and the smugglers of today are no different. For every package of drugs he brought across, countless lives would be ruined.

CHAPTER 17

MIKE

Every now and again, an inmate would appear on the wing looking scared and confused. This was the telltale sign of a 'first-timer' – a new arrival to the prison system. Whereas most prisoners swaggered around the jail as if they owned the place, those who had never been inside before kept their eyes down and tried to spend as much time in their cells as they possibly could. They stuck out like sore thumbs and presented themselves as easy targets – myself included.

When Mike first came on the wing, he looked terrified. His eyes were like saucers and he tried his hardest to assimilate himself into the prison population. He had his hair cut short, talked about the various fights he had been in and loudly proclaimed his hatred for nonces and grasses. Luckily for him, he knew one of the other inmates – a disgraced prison guard serving a five-year sentence for supplying cocaine. This was good in some ways but bad in others – most of the inmates were willing to overlook the fact that this guy had been a screw but there were still some who looked on him with disdain. On one hand, Mike had someone to introduce him to the other cons, but, on the other, he ran the risk of being labelled a 'screwboy' – a prisoner who is overfamiliar with the guards.

At first, people didn't really pay Mike any attention. He was just another new arrival. After a while the news of what he was in for began to spread around the wing. The rumour was that he was serving a sentence for a homophobic hate crime. A good proportion of the jail were homophobic themselves but drew the line at attacking people based on their sexuality. 'He's picked on a weak target,' one of the drug dealers from Hull ranted. 'He's smacked some poof who can't defend himself.' It was beginning to look as if all Mike's efforts had been in vain. The other prisoners were starting to turn against him. 'He's a wrong 'un, that Mike is,' one of the older criminals warned me. 'Stay away from him.'

The prison population were very easily influenced by one another. If someone decided that they didn't like one of the new inmates, countless other cons would instinctively latch onto their dislike for them. Before long, Mike was Public Enemy Number One. The other inmates would gossip behind his back and provide each other with exaggerated accounts of the crime he had committed. He was quickly becoming the black sheep of the wing.

Mike didn't do anything to ease the situation. One of

the unwritten prison rules was that everyone sat in the same seat every day for dinner. Unaware of this, he plonked himself down in another inmate's seat. This was met with looks of disapproval from the surrounding tables.

'What are you doing in my seat?' The owner of the seat had arrived to find another man already sitting at his place. Mike was still under the misguided impression that, if he was to back down to anyone, he would be seen as an easy target. This was true in certain situations but not where it contravened the conventions of prison culture. 'I can sit wherever I want,' he retorted. The rightful owner of the seat explained in precise detail what would happen to him if he carried on sitting there. He quickly moved along to the next table.

Later that day, Mike was minding his own business walking round the yard when one of the black inmates came bounding over. 'Oi, blood!' he shouted. 'Don't I know you from somewhere?' Mike shook his head, but the nervous look in his eyes suggested he wasn't being entirely honest. The other inmate gave him the benefit of the doubt and walked away. There was definitely something that he was keeping from the rest of the wing.

The next day, the same black inmate walked over to him. 'Are you trying to take me for a mug?' he asked him. Before he had time to reply, Mike was punched hard in the side of the head and stumbled back onto the spit-covered concrete floor. 'Quick, get up before the guards see you!' Mike got up and ran back to the wing. 'What was that about?' I asked.

'He's a wrong 'un,' his attacker explained. 'He punched up this girl I know a while back.' So, as well as being a homophobe, Mike was a woman beater. Although hitting girls is not one of the main taboos in British prisons, there are still a good number of inmates who take exception to it. He had been on the wing for only a few weeks and had already marked himself out as an outsider.

I felt sorry for Mike. He had done some bad things, but, then again, so had most of the other prisoners. People like Willy and Smalls had done a lot worse than he had. The difference was that he was a newcomer – nobody knew him and the only information the other inmates had to go on was the fact that he had beaten up a girl and a gay man. There was nothing to suggest that the gay man would have been less able to defend himself than a heterosexual man, but the prisoners had a very stereotypical view of sexuality.

'I smacked the poof,' Mike told me that afternoon. 'It wasn't 'cause he was a poof, though – I didn't even know he was gay.' I thought it best not to ask him about the girl. But it was doubtful that he would have been convicted of a hate crime without proof that his offence had been a targeted attack. Still, punching someone hardly deserved being stigmatised by the other prisoners.

A few hours later, I saw Mike in the guards' office having a long, drawn-out conversation with one of the officers. It didn't pay to be seen talking to the screws so soon after he had been attacked. He wasn't doing himself any favours. 'What was all that about?' I asked him when he had finally finished. 'I've told them that I want moving to another wing,' he told me. 'I don't feel safe here. People are following me round the yard.' Everyone walked around the yard in a circle, so in fact everybody was following everybody else. His statement was clearly ridiculous but at the same time understandable, given the amount of hostility towards him.

The next day, I was woken by the unmistakeable sound of a heavy metal door being slammed open. I could hear Mike's voice and that of one of the screws. 'Get your things,' the screw told him. 'You're heading over to E Unit.' I wondered how he would fare on the notorious E Unit. He couldn't do much worse than he had done on our wing.

Within a few hours of his transfer, Mike had managed to make enemies. He sat in another inmate's place – again. Perhaps he assumed that there were different rules on different wings. Whatever the reason, it got him off to a bad start – it doesn't pay to go against the grain when you are living among violent criminals. Conformity is the key to an easy life.

Soon the rumours about Mike began to drift across to E Unit – but by this stage they had been exaggerated beyond recognition. He was now officially a grass – another inmate had seen him talking to the screws. He hadn't mentioned any names and he had done nothing that constituted telling tales in any way, shape or form. The fact of the matter was that the other prisoners didn't like him and were willing to believe anything negative that they were told about him.

LOWLIFE

A grass is the worst thing you can be in British prisons. It is a step below a rapist or a paedophile. Whereas woman beaters were shunned by a select few, informers were hated by everyone. No one on the wing would have anything to do with him and he was gossiped about at every available opportunity. Every time he went to sit down for dinner, the other prisoners would refuse to have him at their table. They didn't want to be seen to be associating with a grass.

After weeks of being ostracised, Mike finally snapped under the pressure. He took the blade out of his shaving razor and sliced himself across the wrists with it. He had been victimised ever since he arrived in the prison and there was only so much he could take. His cellmate pressed the emergency buzzer and he was rushed to the medical unit. The gash was fairly shallow – it was more indicative of a cry for help than a genuine suicide attempt. It was the sign of a desperate man.

Mike was moved onto G Unit, a special wing for prisoners who found it difficult to cope. I never saw him again – he didn't come out on the yard and avoided any activities that he had to leave the wing for. He had entered the jail full of braggadocio tales of pub fights and bar brawls in a desperate attempt to fit in with the rest of the population. He would leave a broken man.

British jails are filled to the brim with hypocrisy and double standards. If the other prisoners want to victimise someone, they will find an excuse for doing it. It is a system whereby the weak are punished more than the strong – the more respected prisoners can do as they like, whereas the cautious first-time offenders are at the mercy of public perception. The reaction to Mike's crime could have easily been 'good on him, he hit a poof' – several of the other inmates were very vocal in their opposition to homosexuality. But they singled him out as a scapegoat, just as they had done with Wingy.

Mike's situation was a stark reminder of the way in which the prison system operated. If the other inmates had suddenly turned on me, it could easily have been me heading off to G Unit. I made a mental note to be polite and humble at all times. Something as innocuous as sitting in the wrong place at mealtime could lead to the whole wing changing their attitude towards me. In jail, reputation is everything. A few wrong moves can mean the difference between an easy sentence and an unbearably hard one.

CHAPTER 18

SAMMO

For every victim on the wing, there was a predator. Among the most feared of these predators were those that preyed upon their own kind: crooks who stole from crooks. These people were known as 'taxmen' and evoked mixed feelings among their fellow inmates. Some hailed them as morally upright, forced into a life of crime but unwilling to prey upon the innocent. Others believed in honour among thieves and saw them as the lowest of the low.

Sammo didn't give a damn how the other inmates perceived him. He had been on the wing for only a few weeks and already he was causing quite a stir. He was a gambler. He liked to spend his spare time playing cards but seldom seemed to win. Every time he lost a game he would play double or quits and lose again. Eventually he ended up gambling everything he owned and more. He lost. It was now time to pay up. 'You're not getting a thing,' he sneered. 'You can't force me to pay.' This was a bold move. He owed a large amount of tobacco to a Somalian inmate and the black prisoners tended to stick together. He could have put himself in very deep waters.

The wing was awash with rumours that Sammo was going to get 'banged'. Normally at this point anyone with any sense would have placed themselves down the segregation unit for fear of being stabbed or hit with a pool ball in a sock. Sammo stayed put and in the end, nothing happened to him. He had called their bluff and come up trumps. Maybe the word had spread about what he was in for. He was a violent man and he was scared of no one – his criminal record attested to that.

The first time I spoke to Sammo I found him very intimidating. He had a constant expression of anger plastered across his face and looked as if he could snap at any time. 'You're not from an estate, are you?' he asked me, though it was more of a statement. 'No,' I replied, worried that he might now see me as a victim now he was onto the fact I was middle-class. 'Is this your first time in?' I nodded my head. 'You'll be OK. I remember my first time – I was only 15!' This seemed to be a fairly standard age for inmates to receive their first sentence. It was still young to have done something worthy of being locked up for, though.

'I was brought up in care homes,' Sammo explained. 'I was an angry kid growing up in the system. I got put into care when I was eight and ended up getting moved

SIMON EDDISBURY

around to over 30 different homes.' This must have
been deeply unsettling. It meant that just as he got to
know one set of people he was uprooted and moved in
with a completely different group. 'How come you got
put into care?' I asked him, wondering if this was a
sensitive subject that should perhaps be left alone. 'I
burgled a house. My mum couldn't cope.' He had been
put into care at age eight, so he must have burgled the
house when he was even younger. 'Yeah, I started
young,' he laughed. 'The door was open so I just went
in. I only took a few bottles of pop!' This was hardly a
terrible crime. I was beginning to gain some insight
into how he had got to be the way he was.

Sammo's formative years were a familiar story. He
grew up in a broken home on a rundown council
estate. Burnt-out cars and boarded-up houses lined the
streets, and the local children saw TWOCing as an
endless source of amusement. 'West Marsh was a
terrible place to grow up,' he sighed. 'It was awful.
Worst place in Grimsby.'

'What was your first sentence for, then?' I asked him.
'Fighting,' he told me. 'I can't even remember what it
was over. I'd had a few nickings before then for the same
thing, though. I got my first caution at 13.' His first time
inside had been difficult. He was in HMP Wetherby
back in the times when inmates weren't allowed TVs or
CD players in their cells. He had found it mind-
numbingly boring but in a lot of ways very similar to the
care homes he had been in. 'It wasn't hard, it was just a
bit shit,' he told me.

'Was that the first thing you did or the first thing you got caught for?' I asked. He smiled. 'When I was 14 I had a few mates who were into taxing. They'd find a dealer's house, get a firm together and go take their cash.' This sounded like risky business for a group of 14-year-olds to be involved in. 'Did they have any weapons?' He surely must have had something just in case. 'Sometimes,' he told me. 'Some jobs they'd have knives and bats but some they'd go unarmed.' It must have been very dangerous with nothing for protection. 'Strength in numbers,' he explained. 'They'd go in 10 or 20 strong. Even if a dealer is tooled up, he's not going to take out that many people.'

'What got you into taxing, then?' I was curious to know how he had become involved in such a hazardous activity at such a young age. His only previous crimes had been fairly petty and it seemed like a big jump. 'At first it was just through being angry all the time. I was an angry youth. I needed a way of letting it out.' So he hadn't even really been in it for the money? 'Obviously the money was good as well,' he laughed. 'When I got a bit older drugs and drink were the main reason I carried on doing it. I was taking Vallies [Valium] and they make you feel invincible, I'm telling you.' I'd heard similar stories from a few of the high-level criminals on the wing. Those who did violent, face-to-face crimes were often under the influence of Valium. It gave them something of a God complex and made them feel as though there were no consequences to their actions.

Sammo was 15 when he first discovered drugs. It started off with ecstasy and soon progressed to Valium and cocaine. Although not addicted to a single substance, he was drunk or high seven days a week. He would drink six or seven cans of Stella Artois every day as part of his standard routine. It was his way of dealing with the pressures of life. He was sick of feeling depressed and angry so he would blot out his emotions with drink and drugs. Rather than calming him down, this only served to fuel his underlying rage. He would get into fights whenever the opportunity presented itself and he had four convictions for actual bodily harm, two for affray, one for grievous bodily harm and one for wounding with intent.

'The charge I'm in on at the moment is for cutting someone's ear off.' He was the third inmate I had met who was in for this. One had sliced a rival gang member's ear off with a broken bottle and another had cut the ears off a known paedophile and flushed them down the toilet.

'What happened?' I asked him. 'I broke into this guy's house while he was asleep and was gonna rob him. I thought I'd have the element of surprise 'cause it was the middle of the night. I was creeping up on him to grab him when he woke up and went for his machete.' This was an occupational hazard. Dealers often sleep with guns or machetes by the side of their bed. 'I managed to get to it before he did and sliced him with it. I cut him down the side of the head and peeled his ear off. I've never seen so much blood in my life but I was Vallied up at the time, so it didn't really bother me.' It seemed strange that a prescription drug could have such an extreme effect on a person's thoughts. He had cut part of someone's face off and remained completely unfazed by it. 'That's the problem with the Vallies – you have no inhibitions at all. With the coke and the pills you feel confident but you still have your limits.'

It sounded like a scary drug to take and I wondered just how much he had been taking. 'A lot,' he grinned. 'How much did the guy have in the end?' I asked, wondering if the amount from the robbery justified the horrific act of violence he had committed. 'Not that much,' he said. 'He was only selling skunk. You get a lot more from a crack or a smack dealer.' Although skunk is a Class A drug, it is considered to be fairly mild compared with the likes of cocaine or heroin. Selling skunk was not something worthy of being slashed with a machete for. It made me think about my own crime and how stupid I had been. If someone like Sammo had heard about what I had been up to I could have easily ended up in serious trouble. In some ways, it was a good thing that I had been caught sooner rather than later.

Sammo was given an indeterminate sentence with a recommended tariff of two and a half years. He was 18 at the time of his offence and is now in his mid-twenties. In order to facilitate a timely release on an IPP (in the interest of public protection) sentence, a prisoner needs to be on their best behaviour. Inmates serving these sentences are released at the prison's discretion. Sammo was hardly a model prisoner. Rumours were circulating that he was hooked on Subutex, and he was caught with two mobile phones during the time that I was on the wing with him. 'I need to calm down,' he admitted. This was an understatement. 'I'm going to get a job when I get out. I'm going to have to – I'll be on life licence.' It seemed as if IPPs were the most effective form of sentencing – they forced offenders to go straight by placing their lives at the mercy of the prison system. 'I think if I stop drinking and taking as many drugs I can make a go of it,' he told me.

Sammo was not a career criminal. Although the money was a bonus, it was not the reason he became a taxman. He enjoyed the violence and the sense of power that he gained from taking from other criminals. He had spent all his adult life and a good number of his teenage years behind bars. Perhaps it was an attempt to mirror the conditions in which he had grown up. In many ways, being in jail was just like being in care. They had the same forms of entertainment available – pool and TV. There was the same communal atmosphere and the same distrust of authority. For him, jail was very similar to the environment in which he had spent most of his life.

CHAPTER 19

SCOUSE

For every shark behind bars there is also a minnow. For every big-time gangster there is a drug runner, shoplifter or ASBO (antisocial-behaviour order) breacher. Scouse fell within the first two minnow categories. He had no illusions of grandeur and did not succumb to posturing and bravado as the other inmates did – he just got on with things and did what he had to do. He had been a bit of a nuisance to those who made an honest living, but he had never stabbed or shot anyone and didn't intend to.

Scouse was characterised by his wide cheeky grin. This was unusual on a wing with so many screwed-up faces. He'd had a rough life but wasn't one to let it get him down. The only time I saw him get mildly annoyed was when people took the mickey out of him for being Scouse. 'I'm not Scouse – I'm from Runcorn, it's in Cheshire!' he would point out time and time again.

'We've had an education where I'm from!' To me he sounded Scouse, but, then again, Runcorn is a new town for Liverpool and a large proportion of its residents originate from there. He would just have to accept that no one on the wing could tell the difference between Scousers and Runcornians.

There is a popular misconception that everyone who lives in Cheshire is posh. Although the county as a whole is fairly well off, there are still pockets of deprivation throughout. Most of Runcorn fits into this bracket. Known locally as Scumcorn, it became notorious for high levels of teenage pregnancy after appearing in the BBC documentary *Britain's Youngest Grandma*. Crime, unemployment and poor housing are all major issues there and among the worst areas in all of these respects is a place called Halton Brook.

This was where Scouse had grown up and it had more than its fair share of social problems. Gangs of youths hung out on street corners drinking and taking drugs, and it was definitely not the leafy, middle-class Cheshire of popular perception. It had more in common with inner-city Liverpool than Knutsford or Alderley Edge. Growing up in the Brook was pretty grim – not only due to the levels of crime and poverty but also because there was nothing to do. The only form of entertainment for miles around was the youth club, which provided the local youngsters with pool tables and organised activities to keep them out of trouble.

'It was good that place – until we burgled it!' This was the problem with working with kids from deprived backgrounds – most of them were law-abiding and saw the club as something of a safe haven, but others didn't care if they ruined things for everyone else. Scouse liked to get pissed before attending the youth club – just to make the experience a little more interesting. That night he was particularly intoxicated and drunkenly decided to rob the tuck shop. He'd hidden in the toilets at closing time and let his friends in through the back door. They had then booted the doors off the room where the crisps and sweets were kept and helped themselves to everything they could carry.

'I was only 14 – it was just a stupid, pissed-up, spur-of-the-moment thing,' he explained. After being spotted leaving the building clutching a box of Wotsits, he had been arrested and received his first police caution. 'It was nothing,' he told me. 'Just a tellin' off, really.' So had he learnt his lesson? 'Well, I didn't get into any more trouble until four years later, so it must have done something!'

The next time Scouse fell foul of the law, he was 18 and had just moved into a flat of his own. He was socialising with a few friends when there was a loud knock at the door. 'We were banging out the tunes and we nearly didn't even hear it. I opened it up and this busy [policeman] was stood there. I thought, Shit! What have I done now, lad?' The officer had received complaints about the noise and had come round to tell them to keep it down. He smelled cannabis fumes and spotted £30 worth of speed laid out on a nearby table. 'What have we got here then, lads?' he asked them.

'He got an eighth of weed and a few grams of whiz off

us. I got another caution for it.' This was a slap on the wrist. Speed is a Class B drug and the penalties for possession are fairly light, despite the fact that it is highly addictive and can lead to a whole host of mental and physical problems. 'I bet the neighbours were buzzing,' he laughed. 'As far as they were concerned, it served us right for being a bunch of noisy gets!'

Amphetamines were rife in Runcorn at the time. They were cheap, easily available and could be taken orally with no need for complicated preparation procedures. 'We were all doing 'em back then. There was a lot of cash to be made from 'em. By the time I got to 21 I needed an income – I wasn't a kid any more,' he explained. 'I had this "friend" who was selling whiz outside the local shops. He was putting out a bit of weed as well.'

Scouse had started out selling to his immediate peer group and gradually branched out. He had few qualifications and no legitimate means of earning. For him, crime was the obvious path. He would travel into Toxteth every weekend and buy a small amount of each substance to sell. At this stage, he was earning petty cash – just enough to keep him fed and make sure he had enough drugs of his own.

Speed was the main rave drug at the time. Ecstasy was still fairly rare and had only just come into circulation. Most of his customers would take cheap amphetamines every weekend to provide them with the energy to dance through the night. He had a few customers who were addicts but the majority were recreational users.

At that time, Liverpool was the place to go to get

drugs. The speed in Runcorn was heavily cut and shockingly poor in quality. In Toxteth you could get whatever you wanted. There were Jamaican and Somali dealers in the area around Granby Street and Princes Avenue and white dealers on Park Road and Mill Street. There were even drugs doing the rounds that were still relatively unheard of in Runcorn.

Although heroin was prevalent in the major cities, it was still fairly rare in the smaller towns and villages. This left their inhabitants all the more prone to developing a habit, as they were often unprepared for just how addictive it was. It was spreading like a plague throughout the country, and, although the inner cities were the front line, it wasn't long before it had penetrated every nook and cranny of society. 'The first time I ever tried smack, my mate got given some to take home and try. We'd never come across it before and had no idea what it did.' They were high on speed at the time and hadn't given a second thought to taking a substance that they both knew very little about. They took a knife from the kitchen, put the smack in the centre, heated it up and inhaled the fumes. They were then both violently sick.

'It was awful,' he told me. 'I hated it! I should have stopped there but it was new in Runcorn and I didn't really know how bad it was. Six months later we got some more and did it properly using foil. We were both sick again but it was amazing. I was in a dreamlike state and didn't have a care in the world.' From then on, he would smoke it every single day. 'Addiction creeps up on you,' he told me. Soon his weed and amphetamine business had gone down the pan and he didn't care one bit. He was spending all his time smoking smack and had neither the time nor the inclination to do anything else.

Within a few months, Scouse was completely penniless. He had spent all his money on drugs. 'If I had a choice between eating or buying more gear, I would have chosen the gear,' he confessed. 'That's how it gets you after a while. I was really unhealthy. I was malnourished and I wasn't taking care of myself. It got to the point where I realised that I needed another graft to survive.' His peer group had gradually shifted from potheads and layabouts to beggars and thieves. In a relatively short space of time, his life had changed dramatically. 'You hand over a tenner for a bag of smack and you're selling your soul, lad. Trust me,' he sighed.

One day, a few of Scouse's friends had suggested that he join them on a shoplifting spree to get some extra drug money. This was not your average naughty-teenager brand of shoplifting. They would walk into a shop, lift up a rack of clothes and walk out with it. If anyone tried to stop them, there were four of them – what could they do? 'We went all over the Northwest in this van with everything we robbed crammed into the back,' he told me. 'We were smoking gear all the way there and all the way back – I'm surprised we didn't crash!' They did a different town or city every day.

Perhaps if he had been a little subtler, he would have

managed to avoid capture. As it was, Scouse ended up doing ten separate jail sentences over a five-year period. Although the maximum sentence for shoplifting was relatively short, he was still spending more time inside than out. Something had to change or the outside world would become nothing more than a brief interlude between jail terms.

'It wasn't hard to see who was making all the money in there,' he told me. 'They had their cells stacked up with food and walked round the yard in big gold chains. They were all in the drugs game – you didn't see anyone going round like that who was robbing clothes shops!' Scouse had sold drugs before, but they were the wrong drugs. All the more successful criminals were selling smack. It was in a different league from cannabis or amphetamines. Each customer would usually buy at least £100 worth a day. 'I figured that if I was going to keep coming back to jail I might as well have some cash to spend in the canteen [prison shop] while I was in there.'

Scouse made a mental note to start selling heroin as soon as he was back on the streets. It was the only way he could make his time in jail vaguely liveable. He was constantly struggling to scrape together enough money to buy tobacco, never mind drugs. There was no point in doing crime if he was to spend half of his life living in squalor.

When he got out, he knew what he had to do. He needed to save his money and buy his drugs in bulk – then he could sell on what he had left over. This was easier said than done. Anything that he bought he would smoke. Still, as long as he could earn enough to feed his habit, he was happy for the time being.

Time went by and the drugs made him even more lethargic and unwilling to change – he knew what he had to do but lacked the will to do it. He lived for the moment, and at any given moment all he wanted to do was smoke heroin. It was a catch-22 situation – he was addicted to drugs but at the same time subdued by them to the point where he was unable to earn enough to afford them.

The turning point came at about the time he first started smoking crack. He was at his dealer's house and saw another customer buying what looked to be a bag of white stones. He was curious. He had never been one to shy away from trying new things and thought he would give it a go and see what it was like. 'The minute I smoked my first rock I knew that my life would never be the same again,' he told me. 'It felt like having an orgasm but a hundred times stronger. You never forget your first stone – there's nothing like it.'

From that day on, he was hooked. He tried over and over again to recreate that first high but was unable to do so. It was as much a psychological addiction as a physical one. He craved that first perfect hit again but could never quite reach the same level of intensity. He was constantly striving to reach an unattainable high.

Now that his money was going on both crack and heroin, Scouse was spending twice as much as before. He was struggling. He was barely eating and his ribs were showing. His rent was due and he had no idea how he was going to pay it – he needed to find somebody else who would let him move in with them. If he got himself a housemate then the rent would be shared between the two of them and it would be easier to cope. They could pitch in for his rocks as well.

Crackheads tend to stick together. They have a reputation for being sly and untrustworthy and are often pushed to the borders of society. The only people who will give them the time of day are other crackheads. It was through a shared interest in drugs that Scouse met his housemate – a local addict by the name of Sarah. 'I was round at hers all the time shagging her, so in the end I thought I might as well move in,' he explained. Sarah lived in Kensington – a rundown, crime-infested area of south Liverpool. If he was going to pull his finger out and finally start selling smack and crack, this would be the perfect place to set up shop.

Kensington is characterised by the large numbers of abandoned houses that line the streets. It is like a ghost town – there are roads where nearly every single house is boarded up. Teenage gangs terrorise the few inhabitants who remain there, and crack and heroin addicts are never far away. To Scouse, it was ripe for the picking. Other potential homeowners would have been put off by the hordes of zombie-like junkies who trailed the streets, but he looked at them as potential customers. He had connections who could get hold of large amounts of crack and heroin at relatively short notice and he decided to seize the moment and start selling hard drugs. He knew wholesale dealers in Speke, Halewood and Toxteth – all relatively close. All he had to do now was put the word around Kensington that he was the man to come to for drugs and he would be sorted.

And so Scouse established himself as a low-level crack and heroin dealer. He was one of many, as Kensington had no shortage of crooks living there. Putting out drugs was less work than shoplifting had been, but it would have been easier if he had a car. 'I was doing drop-offs round Kenny and the city centre on foot,' he told me. 'Most people bought a bit of both – they had a few rocks and then did some gear to help them with the comedown. Two white, one brown was the standard order!'

'Twelve white and ten brown.' This was a large amount of drugs to be buying in one go. It was like ten deals in one. Scouse had been selling for a few months and he was just beginning to get a feel for it. It seemed suspicious but at the same time he couldn't help thinking how much money he would have coming in if it turned out to be a legitimate deal. 'Where do you want it delivered to?' he asked. The address was in Kenny, only a few streets away. It was tempting. His mouth was watering thinking of all the crack and heroin he could buy with the proceeds. He grabbed his coat, pushed the drugs down the front of his trousers and set off to meet them.

As he waited, Scouse grew increasingly apprehensive. He had a bad feeling about this one. It seemed too good to be true, but by this point he was fixated on how many bags of drugs he would to be able to smoke if everything went according to plan. He glanced to the right. There was no one there. He glanced to the left. There were two hooded youths walking towards him and they appeared to be carrying weapons. 'That was when I knew for sure that I was going to get done over. One of them had a weightlifting bar and the other had a big chunk of wood. The one with the wood smacked me round the head with it and laid me straight out.' When he came round, Scouse was penniless and his drugs were nowhere to be seen.

Whereas someone like Willy or Bolty would have spent every waking minute trying to find out who had robbed them, Scouse put it down to an error of judgement and accepted that he had taken a loss. 'Don't get me wrong,' he told me. 'If I saw them in the street I woulda given them a crack, but there's no point being bitter. I would have probably have done the same to them.' From then on, he was a lot more careful. Anybody buying more than the usual two white and one brown was treated with the utmost suspicion.

'Two white, one brown.' That was more like it. Nothing out of the ordinary – just another deal. He was to bring the drugs to the city centre – it was probably a tramp. 'I'll be with you in about half an hour,' Scouse told him. This time he was sure it was a legitimate customer. He had no grounds for suspicion whatsoever. 'He looked just like a smackhead,' he told me. 'All his teeth were missing and he was stick thin.' As it turned out, he was a copper. Whereas the two hooded youths had stolen his physical possessions, this time three and a half years of his life were to be taken from him.

This was the first sentence he had done for drugs. He

may have earned more money than he would have done from shoplifting but he had also got himself a substantially longer stint behind bars.

Scouse was taken to HMP Walton, his local prison. 'I knew a load of the lads there,' he said, 'but it's a rough jail. It's not like here, where you can owe someone a pack of burn for weeks on end and get away with it. You try that in Walton and you'll get cut to shreds.' There was also a problem with organised violence. 'All the young lads from Birkenhead and them places would arrange fights between the smackheads. They'd say you two can fight each other and the winner gets a ten-bag. It was like *Bumfights* [a controversial film series created by Indecline Films featuring drug addicts fighting with one another]! None of that really bothered me, though – I just kept my head down and got on with things. The worst thing about that sentence was when Sarah left me. She couldn't wait that long.'

It is common for inmates' girlfriends to leave them when they hear that they have been given a long sentence, but Scouse still felt depressed and betrayed. Sarah had been the one positive thing in his life and, now she had gone, he had nothing. Never one to take the break-up of a relationship lightly, he felt down for days on end and smoked even more smack than usual. To take his mind off her, he decided to start writing to another girl, this time from Toxteth. He had been given her address by one of his friends and before long they were fully fledged pen pals.

Scouse's new girl came to visit him on numerous

occasions throughout his sentence. She was more grounded than Sarah had been. She didn't take any drugs and she didn't really approve of his doing so. Maybe this was the type of girl he needed to keep him on the straight and narrow. When he got out, he had no choice but to move in with her straightaway. He couldn't exactly move back in with Sarah and he had nowhere else to go. 'It was a bit of a ball ache 'cause I couldn't smoke gear in front of her,' he told me. 'I had to do it while she was out. It made me cut down a lot, though – she was a good influence on me.'

Scouse eventually got to the point where he was smoking a few rocks and a £10 bag of heroin on the weekend, and that was it. He no longer needed to do crime to fund his habit and he was living a relatively law-abiding life. For once, things were looking up for him. He was in a loving relationship, he was gradually weaning himself off drugs and he was feeling all the better for it.

'That's when she told me. She said things weren't working out and she didn't want to be with me any more. I was gutted. I had nowhere to live either 'cause the flat was in her name! I packed my bags and moved into a hostel.' This was a bad move. The hostel was populated almost entirely by other addicts. 'I was feeling low and needed something to cheer me up,' he told me. 'Everyone else there was smoking gear so I thought, What have I got to lose? I might as well go at it hard again.'

Rather than continuing to score his drugs in Toxteth,

Scouse started venturing into nearby Wavertree, where he could get cheaper deals. He was feeling depressed and self-destructive. Things had been going so well for him, but now he was right back where he started. The reins were off and he was free to smoke as much as he wanted. Unless there was somebody there to tell him that enough was enough, he would take more and more drugs until there was nothing left to take.

Whereas the dealers in Toxteth had remained somewhat aloof from their clientele, Scouse's new dealer was a lot friendlier. He would invite him in for a chat and a cup of tea and was far more pleasant an option to buy from. It made it all the easier for him to continue on the same downward spiral.

In no time at all, the two of them had built up a rapport. 'He wasn't a bad guy,' he told me. 'Some of 'em would try and talk down to you but he kept things on a level.' After they had built up a degree of trust between them, Scouse was offered a job as a delivery boy. 'He needed someone to drop off some packages and knew that I'd take the rap and wouldn't grass him up if I got caught. After all, I'd probably done more jail than all of his other customers put together!'

Scouse was to deliver packs of crack and heroin to three different locations every week – Scarborough, Norwich and Barrow-in-Furness. It was risky business. There were a few ounces of each drug in every pack – enough to send him away for quite some time. Not having a car of his own, he was forced to make the trips by train. They were long journeys – it took him 11 hours to get to Norwich and back. Still, he got to see a bit of the country and the pay was generous.

Of the three drop-offs, Barrow was a rundown industrial town with little to do or see, and Norwich was a grey identikit city much like any other. Scouse's favourite was Scarborough. There was a holiday atmosphere and a pleasant seaside ambience to the place. 'I could chill out on the beach for the day until it was time to get the train back,' he told me.

Scarborough was also home to a number of heroin addicts. Despite its reputation as a picturesque seaside town, it suffers heavily from seasonal unemployment. During the winter months, many are out of a job and looking for other ways to occupy their time. 'There was this guy Jamie I met there who I used to go and have a smoke with. I'd kip over at his house to save me going back the same day.' Jamie was selling smack to fund his habit. 'It was good 'cause he always had plenty of drugs and we never ran out. For a town of its size, there were a lot of people buying off him.' Scarborough has one of the worst rates of heroin-related fatalities in the country and Scouse's new friend was helping to keep the numbers up.

Eventually, Scouse became fed up with travelling halfway across the country and back every few days and decided to go back to street dealing. Jamie agreed to take him on as an employee and told him that he could keep £200 for every £1,000 that he made. He sold two grand's worth of crack and heroin a day and earned £2,800 a week – all of which went on drugs. He was doing all the work but keeping only a fraction of the profit.

To avoid detection, criminals need to be alert at all times. Heroin dulls the senses. Perhaps if Scouse hadn't been constantly high, he might have been wise to the fact that one of his regular customers was an undercover policeman. As it was, he was completely oblivious. The first he knew of it was when his door was booted off its hinges and the drug squad were shouting for him to keep his hands where they could see them. 'What have we got here, then?' the senior officer had asked him, pointing to half a dozen bags of heroin in an open shoebox beneath his bed. It was like his first drugs offence all over again, only on a completely different scale.

This time he was tried for the more serious charge of conspiracy to supply and sentenced to seven and a half years – half a life sentence. The length of the term reflected the levels of preplanning involved in each sale and took into account the fact that he had been working as part of a larger criminal network.

During his time out on bail, Scouse bought 33 grams of heroin and 38 grams of crack and hid them in his rectum to smuggle them into jail. This was £1,800 worth of narcotics – if the bag was to burst, he would almost certainly overdose and die. He was heading to HMP Hull – a jail with a reputation for being full of junkies. He figured that he could sell drugs in there and make some money to take out. By the end of his first ten days of imprisonment, he had smoked the lot – an average of £180 a day. He couldn't go on like this.

The following morning, Scouse signed himself up for a drugs rehabilitation programme. 'I couldn't keep spending that much on drugs,' he told me. 'It was getting ridiculous. They put me on Subbies to try and get me off the smack.' At least now he wouldn't be paying for anything. The drugs he took would be provided courtesy of the prison.

Soon enough, he had become addicted to Subutex. 'Nowadays, there are easily more people selling Subbies than there are selling smack in these places,' he told me. 'I started buying an extra tablet every week on top of what they were giving me.' He would crush the tablets into a fine white powder and snort them through a piece of rolled-up paper.

Scouse managed to rack up a couple of hundred pounds' worth of debt before he realised that he had a problem and switched to methadone. Nicknamed 'Shrek juice' on account of its sickly green colour, it is provided in liquid form to minimise the potential for selling it on. He was made to drink it in full view of the prison staff, just to make sure he didn't trade it for anything else.

'Soon I won't be on anything at all.' I wanted to believe him. He had taken the first step to recovery but there was still a long way to go. Although the phrase 'once an addict, always an addict' is pessimistic and cynical, in most cases it has the ring of truth to it. The real test would come when he got back into the outside world.

'Where are you going when you get back out, then?' I asked him. 'Back to Runcorn I think,' he told me. 'I miss the place!' It was run down and there wasn't much to do there, but for him it was home. 'Do you reckon you're off the gear for good, then?' He nodded. 'Oh, yeah. I've had enough of that stuff – it's done enough damage. I don't reckon I'm even going to carry on selling it. If I do, I'll stick with the packages – there's not as much chance of getting caught that way. You're not as likely to pass 'em on to an undercover busy.'

'So do you regret what you did, then?' I asked. 'Well, when there's nonces out there raping kids and only getting a few months, do you think I deserve seven years?' He did have a point. 'I haven't hurt anybody directly but I get a longer sentence than if I'd stabbed someone.' It was true. While he was a bit of a wheeler-dealer character, Scouse was not a violent man, yet he had received a longer sentence than people who had done some horrific things.

Scouse had a long time left to go. He was just over halfway through his sentence. 'It's a bad 'un, this one, lad! These four walls have been my world for the last few years!' I couldn't imagine what it would be like to know you'd be stuck within the same surroundings for at least another year. 'Last time you'll see me in a place like this, kidda.' I hoped so. He was harmless enough – if he could just keep off the drugs, he would be in with a chance. Hopefully, this time he would finally break away from them once and for all. Crack and heroin had been his sole motivation, but it was time for something different. It was time for him to live his life the way he should have done from the start.

CHAPTER 20

DEVON

Scouse had done some risky things to get hold of drugs, but there were people who had done far worse. One of the Asian inmates was moved off the wing for supposedly giving a Subutex addict an 8mg tablet in return for oral sex. It takes a desperate man to sell his body for drugs – and a man who has done far too much time in prison to accept the offer.

In American prisons, one inmate in five reports that he has been sexually assaulted during his sentence. I asked Willy, who had probably done more time than the rest of the wing put together, how often things like that happened in this country. 'In some prisons you get rent boys,' he told me. 'It's usually the long-term ones. A while ago, I was in a jail I hadn't been in before and I was just coming off smack. I was sweating all the time, so I spent a lot of time in the showers. One of the older lads came and warned me that if I spent too much time there the rest of the wing would think I was selling my arse. It was how the faggots let the other fellas know that they were up for it.'

At least it was consensual sex in British prisons then. 'Well, not really,' Old Man Steve butted in. 'Have you ever heard of Rufus? He's a big black fella that used to be in Armley – built like Mike Tyson. He drugs his cellmates and rapes them. He's rock solid, so no one will say a word to him. When he gets asked what he's in for he tells them straight – 'I'm a nonce.' There's another black fella from Bradford who does the same thing.' I breathed a sigh of relief that all my cellmates had been fairly normal so far.

Later that day, I talked to one of the older gangsters who had been in a few different long-term jails. 'It does happen,' he told me. 'I remember a few years back I was in one of them places and I walked into this guy's cell without knocking. He had his cellmate bent over the sink and he was slatting one up him. It's not as common as in America, but it does go on.' So, as well as the hazard of random violence, I now had the threat of nonconsensual sodomy to contend with.

The first time I encountered a 'prison gay' I was terrified. I was in the showers when a Jamaican drug dealer serving a 12-year sentence came through the door and introduced himself to me. 'I'm Devon,' he said, looking at me as if I were a piece of meat. 'How's it going?' he asked. 'Not bad,' I told him, stepping out of the showers and moving towards my clothes. 'How are you finding it in here?' he followed up, his gaze fixed upon my naked body. 'It's OK, I suppose.' I was attempting to keep the conversation to a minimum so I could leave the room as quickly as possible. 'It's harder when you've left somebody behind on the outside,' he told me. 'Have you got a wife?' I shook my head. 'What about a girlfriend?' I shook my head again. His eyes lit up. 'What about a boyfriend?' he asked, smiling and licking his lips as he spoke. I threw my clothes on at top speed and darted out of the door.

For the next few weeks, I made sure that Devon was nowhere to be seen before I went in the showers. It was ignorant of me to assume that anybody who was gay in prison would be a rapist, although it is slightly intimidating when a gay man comes onto someone while they are naked – especially if they are serving time for selling crack and heroin. Drug dealers aren't the most moralistic of people – they will take what they want rather than ask for permission.

'What's the deal with that Jamaican guy?' I asked my cellmate as we sat bored behind the door one day. 'He's a battyman [homosexual],' he told me. 'He's harmless enough, though. He got moved here from his last jail 'cause he was getting stick for it.' So he had definitely been propositioning me then – I hadn't imagined it. I considered avoiding the showers altogether but thought better of it, as I still had several months of my sentence left.

Finally the day came when Devon was in the showers at the same time as I was. Oh, well, I thought, I might as well finish washing myself. It was impractical to spend the rest of my time inside avoiding him. 'Wha gwaan?' he asked me in his feminine Jamaican accent. I wasn't exactly sure what 'wha gwaan' meant, never mind how to reply to it. 'Erm, yeah . . . not bad,' I told him. This time he was looking at my face rather than my penis. Perhaps he had lost interest. 'How long have you got left?' I asked – a standard piece of jail conversation. After a few minutes of idle chitchat, I dried myself off and left the room. I had been stressing myself out over nothing. He had ascertained that I was into women, realised that he was barking up the wrong tree and accepted defeat.

'Has Devon been trying it on with you again?' my cellmate joked later that day. 'Nah,' I told him. 'Thank God.' I had one thing fewer to worry about now that the threat of being molested in the showers had subsided. 'He's been trying it on with Little Dave lately,' another inmate piped up, overhearing our conversation. It was impossible to talk about anything without its becoming a group discussion. 'He offered him a pack of burn the other day to move into his cell with him.' Little Dave was another small, skinny prisoner with a similar build to myself. Despite his stature, he was supposedly hard as nails. Devon was treading on dangerous ground. Luckily, Dave was completely oblivious of the fact that he had an admirer. He assumed that he was just being friendly.

It wasn't hard to tell that Devon was gay. He was camp as a row of tents. He was the only gay Jamaican I'd ever come across in my life and he must have had a hard time growing up in such an openly gay-hating country. 'Battymen get bun [burnt] out over there,' my cellmate told me. 'He won't have had it easy.'

As I got to know Devon a little bit better, I felt ashamed of my previous attitude towards him. He was actually a really nice guy. He had been selling crack and heroin in Chapeltown to earn enough money to support his family back home. 'I dunno whether to go back there,' he told me. 'I feel more at home over here now.' I assumed that this was because the British were more accepting of his sexuality. In Leeds there are various gay clubs, societies and venues. In Jamaica, buggery is still illegal and is punishable by up to ten years in prison.

Devon was surprisingly popular on the wing, even among some of the more bigoted inmates. Big Joe, a skinhead BNP supporter from Oldham, would regularly proclaim what a 'sound bloke' he was, despite the fact that he was gay and black. His cellmates weren't always particularly tolerant, though. One of the car thieves refused to be locked up with him after hearing about his sexuality from another inmate. 'I reckon he was a wrong 'un,' Devon told me. 'He's a bit old to be stealing cars and he never talked about his crime.' It was possible that he could have deliberately refused to share Devon's cell, so he would be taken off the unit. Inmates who had committed taboo crimes would often do this when they thought the rest of the wing were onto them.

Devon's next cellmate was an elderly Liverpudlian doing time for aggravated burglary. 'I don't mind that he's gay,' he told me, as he moved his stuff into the cell.

'It's not as if he's got pictures of naked men up on the walls or anything.' Although he claimed to be tolerant, the reality was very different. Those in the neighbouring cells were woken up in the middle of the night by the sound of raised voices. 'You gay, black bastard!' the Liverpudlian was shouting. The guards rushed over to see what all the fuss was about. 'I can't share with him,' he told them. 'Get this queer nigger out of here or I'll do him in.'

The next morning, I went over to Devon's cell to find out what had happened. 'We had an argument,' he told me. 'I wanted to watch TV and he wanted to go to sleep – then he just went mad!' So although he supposedly had no problem with Devon's sexuality, the Liverpudlian was quick to bring it up the minute they had a disagreement. 'Dev's a chilled-out guy,' Joe told me. 'I don't get it. There was no need for that at all.'

The next day, the Liverpudlian was met with cold stares. 'What he did was out of order,' another inmate told me. 'Devon ain't hurting no one.' I was surprised that a gay man was receiving so much support in such a potentially hostile environment. 'He's coming towards the end of a long sentence,' I heard another prisoner saying. 'The last thing he needs is some old fella throwing a divvy fit at him.'

Even the offenders who claimed to be anti-gay were surprisingly tolerant now that they were forced to get to know a homosexual prisoner. Had Devon attempted to be more pushy, things might have been different. As it was, he kept his head down and tried to be as friendly and personable as he could be. He was an inherently likeable inmate regardless of his sexuality – a fact that enabled him to live relatively unhindered, and the majority of the wing were friendly towards him. 'There's a lot worse things to be than a poof in here,' a crack dealer from Hull pointed out. In a place where murderers and rapists were indistinguishable from the general population, being gay was a trivial matter. Some prisoners didn't like gay people, but, then again, a lot more didn't like woman beaters, paedophiles, rapists, granny bashers etc. There was no reason to pick on people for their differences when there were so many genuinely nasty characters lurking in the wings.

Although many prisoners were politically incorrect to an extreme, there were very few extreme racists or homophobes. Words like 'faggot' and 'poof' were used on a daily basis, but, when it came down to it, an inmate's attitude would determine his treatment from the other cons. There were prisoners who voted for the BNP and spouted racist rhetoric at every opportunity but were also best friends with black people. Prison could be a strange and contradictory place. It is easy for someone to hate a group of people they never come into contact with. It is more difficult when they are locked in a confined space with them for hours at a time. Behind bars, there is no stigma attached to prejudice or discrimination. People are free to take a dislike to anybody they want. When faced with the option of being friends with a gay prisoner or a violent psychopath, even the most hardened of homophobe is inclined to opt for the safer option.

With Devon the stereotype of the 'prison gay' as a violent predator couldn't have been further from the truth. He was a little forward, but he was surprisingly relaxed and chilled-out for a crack dealer and I couldn't imagine him hurting anyone. His sexuality must have made his time inside twice as hard. I was pleased that he had been accepted by the other prisoners. He had a few years left to go, but, now that he was in a more accepting environment, it would be downhill all the way.

'I wouldn't recommend selling drugs to anyone,' he told me. 'When I get back to Leeds, I'm going to live my life the way I should have done before.' After being repressed in anti-gay Jamaica, he had been locked away for 12 years once he made it to the UK. When he got out, he would finally be able to live a normal, law-abiding existence. I wished him the best of luck.

CHAPTER 21
PELÉ

There are many different reasons for becoming a criminal. Money. Power. Respect. Then there are the crimes of passion – those born of emotion, whether it be love, hate, jealously or envy. For some it is the love of a woman. For others it is the love of a family member. And for a small but significant minority it is the love of a football team.

Hooliganism is different from all other forms of organised crime in that it is a completely nonprofit activity. It is done by people who genuinely enjoy fighting with one another. There are a few firms who indulge in a bit of shoplifting every now and again or who sell a few drugs on the side, but for the most part it is done for little or no financial reward. It is an activity that has existed since the 1800s and, despite condemnation from officials and players alike, it is still very much alive and kicking.

Whereas some rivalries originate out of the close proximity of two neighbouring teams, others are deeper-rooted. They often represent social or political grudges that have nothing at all to do with football. The rivalry between Chesterfield and Mansfield Town goes back to the days of the miners' strike in the 1980s. Whereas the miners in Derbyshire decided to observe the strike, those in Nottinghamshire chose to carry on working. This led to a deep-seated resentment among Chesterfield's mining population, who labelled them 'scabs' – a derogatory term for strike breakers. It was the worst thing you could be, a stigma like no other.

Pelé was both an avid Chesterfield supporter and an ex-miner. As far as he was concerned, Mansfield were the enemy. They had betrayed their fellow miners and could never be forgiven. 'They are pure scum,' he told me. 'Scabs – down to the very last one of them, mush.' Pelé was something of an anomaly in that he was of mixed race but talked in typical white council-estate vernacular peppered with Romani in a strong, slightly old-fashioned Derbyshire accent.

Pelé grew up in the traditional mining village of Newbold, just outside Chesterfield. He was from a mining family – his father had worked in the mines before him. Although not within the limits of the town itself, Newbold is home to a large number of fanatical Chesterfield supporters. It is a working-class area, typified by its love of the local team. Whereas the vast majority of the fans there were happy to register their support peacefully, there was always a small contingent dedicated to causing trouble. 'You'd see them down the local pubs. They were like an army. They were 10 or 20 strong, all in terrace fashions. They had the girls throwing the fanny at 'em, mush – throwing it.'

The Chesterfield Bastard Squad. The name alone summed them up – they were bastards and proud of it. All heads would turn when they walked into the room – some out of fear and some out of respect. 'They were the best dressed in town. Back then it was Stone Island, Burberry, Aquascutum, Sergio Tacchini, Chipie . . . This was when they all first came out, of course. You shoulda seen the birds they got – some right 'uns, mush.'

At that time, Pelé had been an impressionable 15-year-old boy. He had already got himself into his fair share of scrapes and was looking for a place to prove himself. 'I was hanging out on street corners back then, tryna be a bad boy,' he told me. 'I was always into my boxing and that kept me out of trouble but I was lucky not to have been locked up – I'd already had a few close 'uns.' One of these close 'uns had been a wounding-with-intent charge for stabbing a joyrider who had bumped into his mother's car. He had taken it to trial and received a verdict of not guilty – a narrow escape, as he could have ended up spending four years in a young offenders' institution.

'The thing with hooligans was that no one would go to the cops,' he explained. It was consensual violence. Both sides knew what they were letting themselves in for. It seemed like the perfect way to channel his youthful aggression without landing himself in a police cell.

Race, however, was a big issue. This was perhaps to be expected, as hooliganism is a stereotypically white, working-class crime. 'A lot of the lads didn't want me around 'cause I was-mixed race. I used to look up to my cousin 'cause he was fully black but had still managed to get their respect. He'd come round my gran's house after the match days covered in injuries and tell us all his war stories.' Pelé was desperate to follow in his cousin's footsteps: he saved up all his money and bought himself a Sergio Tacchini tracksuit. 'There was some that were impressed but a lot just gave me dirty looks as if to say: who's he to be wearing that? It was time for me to prove myself on the terraces.'

'Arm yourself up,' Pelé's cousin had told him. 'We're going to war.' He was still only 16 and he was preparing for his first taste of inter-firm warfare. 'I got myself a craft knife from the market. That was what they were using back then – just a little Stanley blade. You don't really wanna take something that's gonna kill someone and end up doing life. You just want something you can slash the surface of their skin with and mark 'em up a bit.'

Pelé was handy with his fists – he had been boxing since he was seven years old and he was the Derbyshire schoolboy champion. He had used knives before but was by no means an expert. 'I was on edge,' he told me. 'I didn't know what to expect. I'd been in fistfights before and I'd used the odd weapon, but it wasn't the same.' It was a home game against Walsall – a 2–2 draw. But it wasn't the match that was important. It was what came afterwards.

'We walked round to where the coaches were parked and they had a little firm there waiting for us. Nothing major and nothing too organised – just a few lairy beer-monster types.' This should have been no problem but they put up more resistance than expected. 'There was only a few of us there and my cousin was getting overpowered. This big hulk of a man was kicking him all over the place.' Keen to show willing, Pelé ran round the back and slashed the man down the side of his face. 'I peeled his ear clean in two and he dropped to his knees screaming. I'm telling you now, gadge – I got that much of a rush that I got an actual physical erection. I was a 16-year-old boy – the thought that I could take a grown man down like that had me buzzing my tits off.'

And so he became a fully fledged member of the Bastard Squad. He had drawn the blood of a rival supporter and shown that he was willing to fight for his team. There were still those who doubted him but this was mainly down to his race. 'Some of them thought that there was only room for one black guy in the firm. They weren't full-on racist but they were definitely borderline, mainly the older members, though – the younger ones weren't as bad.'

It was during a clash with the Squad's arch enemies Mansfield that Pelé finally gained the respect of the older members of the firm. He was drinking at a Mansfield pub when several of their fans started laying into a high-ranking Chesterfield hooligan. There were seven Chesterfield fans and around 20 Mansfield fans –

things weren't looking good. This was his chance to prove that he was willing to fight against the odds. It was his chance to shine. 'Our top boy was getting stomped all over by at least four of the scabs. We had a few hundred lads in the town but they were all in different pubs. I thought, I'm not having this, so I grabbed a bottle of whisky and smashed the biggest guy in his head with it. There was blood coming out of his nose and his ears and the floor was soaking with it. After that no one ever mentioned my race again. I finally got the respect I deserved.'

From that moment on, Pelé was accepted into the inner circle. 'I was endorsed by the top boys,' he grinned. 'No one could say a thing to me. Word spread around about me and they wanted me for all the major clashes from then on. I got some right fanny as well – the hooligans had their own groupies called "hoolie birds". They loved the fact I was black 'cause a lot of 'em had never been with a black lad before.' His race was finally beginning to work in his favour.

'Were you in it for the women, then?' I asked him. 'Nah, it was the sense of loyalty. Like, we were all brothers in arms, all wearing the same brands of clothes like it was a uniform. I liked the closeness of it – the unity. It was like an army, mush.' It seemed to me that he had been attracted to the sense of belonging that it had given him and that he had used his involvement in football violence to try to counteract any hang-ups that he may have had about his race. 'There is that to it,' he told me. 'I always felt like I was the odd one out. Chesterfield is a very white town and I suppose I felt like I was looking for somewhere to fit in.'

'Have all your sentences been for violence?' I asked. 'Every last one of them!' he replied. 'I'm not a thief or a drug dealer – I'm a fighter. Although I'm not even that any more – I just want a quiet life when I get out of here.' What had given him the sudden change of heart? There had clearly been a time when he lived for clothes, women and punch-ups. 'There's another side to it all.' His face straightened up and he stared intensely at the floor. 'It's a lot less glamorous. I've had a lot of bad things happen to me – I've been beaten, stabbed, had my head stamped on . . . The worst of all was when I killed a man. I only hit him once and he was gone. I ended up doing manslaughter for it.' He looked guilty, as if the knowledge of what he had done had been eating him up for all this time and he was finally able to let it all out. 'It's a bad feeling to know that you've taken a man's life. It's something you never forget.'

I had seen Pelé training with the boxing pads – he had a powerful punch. Every time his fist collided with the pads there was an almighty bang like a car hitting a wall. His hands were deadly weapons and needed to be used carefully. He was far too good at what he did to be throwing them around willy-nilly.

'I'm a Christian,' he explained. 'I've done a lot of bad things but it's time for me to turn my life around. God has given us all this beauty and I think it's about time I gave something back.' Pelé was friends with a good number of the wing's black Muslim population, so I was surprised that he had selected Christianity as his religion. Still, I got the impression that he didn't really fit in with the other black inmates, and I had heard several of them criticising him behind his back, saying that he 'talked white' and that he was a 'coconut' (black on the outside, white on the inside). He was in limbo – stuck between two cultures and shunned from both directions.

'Life is like a TV,' he went on. 'Would you read the instruction manual if you'd just bought a new telly?' 'Um, probably not,' I replied. 'See, that's why you're an atheist!' he told me. 'Life is like a TV and the Bible is the instructions to it. If you don't read the manual then you don't know what it's all about. I've read the Bible and I'm a changed man. I know I'm going to heaven when I die, gadge!'

So Chesterfield's very own Cass Pennant had found religion. 'You need to read your instruction manual!' he would tell me whenever he saw me around the wing. He was one of the few inmates who seemed like a genuinely reformed character. Sure, he was still a little rough around the edges but for the most part, he seemed intent on leaving his violent past behind him.

On the day of his release, Pelé was over the moon. 'Get in there, gadge!' he shouted, punching the sky with his fists. Back to Chesterfield. 'The heart of the North', he called it, although it is technically in the Midlands. 'The next time there's a match on I'll be there for the football and nothing else. This is the last time you'll see me in a place like this.'

A few weeks passed and I waited with bated breath to

hear if Pelé had managed to stay on the straight and narrow. He had promised to write to a few of the other inmates and I was curious to see if he would be able to keep himself out of trouble.

'Pelé's back in!' Eh? Surely he wasn't back inside already! 'What happened?' I asked. 'Licence recall. He missed his probation.' For all his talk of moving on with his life, Pelé had failed at the first hurdle. I felt shocked and slightly disappointed that he had let himself down like this. I could see no logical reason why he would have failed to turn up, but it was an all-too-familiar story. Serial offenders often find it difficult to abide by any rules whatsoever and are recalled to prison within a couple of weeks of getting out. It must have been a crushing feeling to have been set free only to be arrested and imprisoned again straight afterwards. Maybe next time he would make a proper go of it. For now, he had a lot of time in which to reacquaint himself with his life manual.

CHAPTER 22
DUTCHY

All Pelé's convictions had been for violence, but there was another hooligan on the wing with convictions for pretty much everything. Attempted murder, firearm possession, drug dealing – you name it, he'd done it. He wasn't one to restrict his aggression to the terraces and he was serving a sentence for armed robbery and possession of three different firearms.

Dutchy was called Dutchy because he was Dutch. It wasn't a very imaginative nickname. He wasn't *fully* Dutch, either: he was half Dutch and half Algerian. His mother was a Dutch Catholic and his father was an Algerian Muslim – he had grown up going to the mosque one week and the church the next. His parents were determined to raise him in both cultures so as not to neglect his dual heritage. Despite their efforts to raise him with the morals of both faiths, however, he had been heavily involved in crime from the age of ten years old.

Dutchy grew up in Slotervaart, one of the poorest boroughs in Amsterdam. It has a significant immigrant population – approximately 33 per cent Moroccan, 21 per cent Turkish and 5 per cent Surinamese – and it has been the site of a number of high-profile race riots. It has also made the news for a series of violent incidents, including the fatal stabbing of a 16-year-old schoolboy during an argument with a classmate over ownership of a pen. 'There's worse areas than Slotervaart,' Dutchy told me. 'It gets a lot of bad press but most of the time it's fairly quiet.'

In the late 1960s and early 1970s, large numbers of Moroccans arrived in the district looking for work. They were originally referred to as 'guest workers', the idea being that they would return to their country of origin when they were no longer needed. No efforts were made to teach them the language and there was little attempt to integrate them into mainstream society. Little wonder, then, that the area developed so many social problems a few decades down the line.

'There's a lot rougher areas of the city to live,' Dutchy went on. 'Most of the kids I hung about with weren't even from Slotervaart. It just got a bad rep 'cause it was an immigrant area. They didn't understand the culture. Besides, we did most of our crime around the coffee shops in the centre.' At just 10 years old, he and 20 of his friends would gather outside the cannabis cafés waiting for the tourists to come out. The oldest member of the gang was a mere 13 years old, and they were armed to the teeth with knives and coshes. 'We used to buy our weapons from this guy outside a shop called the Old Man. There were always dodgy people hanging about outside the coffee shops – you could buy anything you wanted from them at any age.' The minute the tourists stepped out of the shops and into the streets, they were set upon. 'We were crazy back then. It was all Algerian and Moroccan kids – a lot of them from poor areas. These foreigners would come out smashed from smoking weed and unable to walk straight. We'd beat them up and take their money.'

When he was 12, Dutchy and his friends decided to rob a local money launderer and things went badly wrong. They surrounded him in his own home, threatened him with knives and made off with a large sum of money. They assumed that this was the last that they would hear of it, but they had gravely underestimated his capabilities. He had eyes and ears all over the city and quickly managed to locate them. 'We were just young kids,' he explained. 'We thought we were invincible. We didn't think that anything we did could come back on us.' If he had been a fully grown man, he could well have ended up dead for what he had done. Because he was barely in his teens, he managed to get away with a beating, but it was still a cause for concern for his conservative Muslim father. Worried that his son would get himself into serious trouble, he sent him off to Algeria to keep him out of harm's way.

'I just saw it as a holiday, really,' he grinned. 'I got to see a bit of the world. It didn't change me at all, though. The first thing I did when I got back was get myself two ounces of coke on tick and a 6mm pistol.' He was still only 13 years old – too young to have sex or smoke cigarettes legally, yet here he was buying guns and Class A drugs. 'I took the coke into school and shifted it in no time at all. After a while, I started diversifying into weed and ketamine as well.' Ketamine is a horse tranquilliser that causes hallucinations. Users report a feeling of complete detachment from the physical world and long-term use can lead to severe psychological damage. Suffice to say, it is a substance that should be kept away from 13-year-old boys at all costs.

Eventually, Dutchy was caught selling drugs on the playing field and promptly excluded from school. He was lucky he hadn't had his gun on him. As all of his main customers were school pupils, he had effectively been stripped of both his livelihood and his education in one fell swoop. His parents went ballistic but there was nothing that they could have said or done to dissuade him from selling drugs. 'I was addicted to the excitement,' he told me. 'I loved it.'

Now that he was no longer in school, Dutchy needed a new turf on which to sell his wares. The coffee shops seemed like a good place. If people were smoking weed there was a good chance that they would be willing to take other drugs as well. Within no time at all, he was back in business and putting out cocaine, ecstasy, PCP and acid.

Dutchy prided himself on his people skills. Whereas many of the other dealers would talk down to their customers and treat them with contempt, he was professional and personable at all times. 'It's important to build up a rapport with your clients,' he told me. 'Without them, you would be broke. I treated them like they were my friends and I was always getting invited to parties and nights out with them. That was what first got me into the hooligan scene – I used to sell to a few guys from the F-Side and they had asked me if I wanted to go to a match with them.'

The F-Side is a term used to describe the most fanatical of Ajax's supporters. The name was originally given to a group of season-ticket holders who occupied the F section of the stadium directly behind the goal, but it is now used to refer to the many hooligans who follow the club.

Dutchy accepted their offer and was mesmerised by the sheer intensity of the F-Side's support for their team. 'It was amazing!' he told me. 'They were the most hardcore supporters you could imagine. I fell in love with the camaraderie and the loyalty straightaway.' One of the F-Side's unusual characteristics was their pro-Semitic stance. They referred to themselves as 'the Jews' after the city's sizeable Jewish population (who lived in the east of the city, where the club was founded), and they were often to be seen carrying flags bearing the Star of David to their matches. 'We were holding up Israeli flags and chanting "Joden, Joden [Jews, Jews]" and then, after the match, that was when it really got good.'

Dutchy had enjoyed the chanting and the flag waving, but it was the post-match festivities that really got his juices flowing. 'That was when I realised just how much I loved to fight,' he told me. 'It was like an all-out war. There was people getting stabbed, whipped with bike chains, hit with bottles . . . you name it.' From that point on, he stood in the F section at every Ajax game and swore his allegiance to the Joden. 'I liked the football, but I loved what happened afterwards!'

Time went by and hooliganism gradually became a way of life. 'It was like a community. There were around 200 to 300 people in the firm, but about 25 that I hung around with. We were friends as well as allies and we'd go out grafting together as well.' Gradually, his group of friends began to consist entirely of other hooligans to the point where he was no longer hanging around with his old childhood gang. 'It was mostly white guys. There were a few Moroccans and Algerians as well.' Unlike Pelé, Dutchy was never made to feel uncomfortable on account of his race. 'It wasn't an issue,' he told me. 'So long as you were Ajax, you were accepted.'

At the age of 14 he suffered his first serious injury. He was stabbed in the arm with a kitchen knife and ended up on a life support machine. 'Didn't that make you want to pack it all in?' I asked. Towards the start of my sentence I would have been shocked that someone was willing to stab a 14-year-old boy over a football rivalry. By this point, I just took it in my stride. 'Nah,' he replied. 'It just made me realise that I had to carry a tool of my own to protect myself with. I'd always gone unarmed but from then on I took a hook knife with me.'

At 15, Dutchy received his first stint behind bars. He had thrown a Molotov cocktail into the opposing crowd and was given a three-month custodial sentence. 'It was at a game against Den Haag. They had quite a good firm but we still laid into them. This copper saw me throwing the petrol bomb and grabbed me and slapped the cuffs on.' So what had his first time in a young offenders' been like? 'It was OK,' he told me. 'Easier than over here, I would say. It didn't put me off doing crime, let's put it that way. It just made me think of more ways to avoid getting caught.'

When he came out, Dutchy shifted his attention from hooliganism back to cocaine. He figured that if he was going to end up back behind bars then it might as well be for something that he could profit from. 'I still had the odd clash here and there,' he told me. 'I always made sure I was there when we played Feyenoord. They were our biggest rivals.' Feyenoord have a number of different firms fighting their corner: the Rotterdam Youth Squad, Rotterdam Hooligans, Lunatics, SCF and FIIR, to name but a few. Just as Ajax has its F-Side, the more fanatical Feyenoord fans are referred to as the S-Side and are equally extreme in their support for their team.

'They were probably the hardest firm in Holland,' Dutchy conceded. 'They had some real mad men.' Feyenoord hooligans were violent whether there had been a match on or not. One time he had unknowingly shaken the hand of an S-Sider during a night out, accidentally revealing the triple-X tattoo on his own hand, signifying his allegiance to Ajax. The Feyenoord fan had immediately whipped out a Stanley knife and gouged it into his hand, attempting to hack the tattoo out of his flesh. He had the scars to prove it.

When Dutchy was 16, his father suggested that he marry the daughter of one of his friends. He figured that having a wife would force Dutchy to settle down and get a proper job. His wife-to-be was a half-Algerian girl he had known from his early childhood. He had always got on well with her, he thought, so why not? It would keep his dad happy and she could help him to bag the coke up.

And so the two of them got married and moved into a house in the Bijlmermeer area of the city. 'That's a real ghetto right there,' he grinned. 'People say Slotervaart is bad but it's nothing compared with the Bijlmermeer.' The Bijlmermeer is an area of high-rise social housing inhabited mainly by the descendents of African and Surinamese immigrants, and it is the centre of Amsterdam's black community. It is also the street-robbery capital of Holland. In 1995 there were 2,000 reported robberies in the area – more than five a day. 'It was crazy back then. There were people getting robbed in broad daylight and quite a few shootings as well.'

One of these shootings was in the middle of the day on a crowded residential street. Two rival factions were letting off shots at each other and Dutchy's wife was unlucky enough to be caught in the crossfire. She fell to the ground screaming in agony. Luckily, she survived, but it was a close call. She was left bearing the scars both physically and mentally.

'Life was cheap. We lived there for two years and then I was drafted into the army,' he told me. 'We had national service at the time. I was relieved to be out of there – and that was saying something because I got sent over to Bosnia!' He was sent over as a UN peacekeeper – ironic given his love of conflict. 'It was hard graft,' he explained. 'We had to be up at the crack of dawn and had some dickhead bellowing orders in our ears every five minutes.' Dutchy was used to being his own boss. He was never one to respect authority and didn't appreciated the strict regime of the Dutch army.

The Dutch peacekeepers have been heavily criticised for their passivity towards the genocide of 8,000 unarmed Bosnian Muslims by the Serb invaders at Srebrenica. 'We were meant to just stand there and let them get loaded into a truck to be taken away and killed. It was women and children as well. I thought, I'm not having this!' Dutchy hadn't liked his commanding officer as it was, and took this opportunity to voice his disdain for him and everything he stood for. An argument ensued and Dutchy struck the officer hard in the face with the barrel of his gun.

'I did the right thing,' Dutchy maintained. 'I've done some sick things but nothing compared to what was happening over there. They were getting massacred.' Whether his actions had stemmed from his unwillingness to stand by and let innocent people die or his general dislike of authority, the end result was the same. He was dishonourably discharged from the military and sent back home to the Bijlmermeer.

'Back to the ghetto!' But things were not the same. His wife had been unable to keep the drugs business going single-handedly during his time away and he had lost all his regular customers. He had expected to go home and pick up exactly where he had left off, but even his relationship with his wife was different. 'I guess you forget that time doesn't stand still when you're away,' he sighed.

Fed up with how life was going in Holland, Dutchy decided he needed a change of scenery. He had family over in the UK and felt that it was time that he paid them a visit. 'I just packed my bags and left,' he told me. 'I had nothing to stay in the Netherlands for and I wanted to see what it was like over here.'

Dutchy moved onto the Orchard Park Estate in Hull. It wasn't exactly what he had expected England to be like. 'It was a shithole! It was like the Bijlmermeer only a hundred per cent white and with more smack and less guns.' It wasn't the best place to live but now that he was there he figured that he might as well make the most of it. He seemed to have assimilated effortlessly into British council-estate culture, and his dialect, slang and patterns of speech were all distinctly East Yorkshire.

Although Orchard Park was home to a large number of drug users, they were at the more undesirable end of the spectrum. Dutchy liked to sell to clubbers and partygoers, not vagrants and smackheads. Still, there was one thing that he liked about the UK, and that was its women. 'There's some right fanny over here,' he told me. 'That was what got me out of Hull. I met this girl Sarah from Morden in London and went down to live with her for a bit.'

Morden is a distinctly average suburb on the southern outskirts of London, but it was a definite improvement upon Orchard Park. London was more Dutchy's scene. It was a livelier city with a higher class of drug taker. 'Obviously, I can't admit to anything that I did since I came over here,' he told me. 'I did a lot of partying, though. I was going to a lot of dance clubs – the types of places where there was a load of charlie getting passed about. And people selling it as well . . .'

All was going well until he bumped into a Jamaican drug dealer who asked him if he could get hold of 10 ounces for him. 'I was dancing away, off my head and he came over and just asked me straight out.' This was a suspiciously large amount of cocaine to be buying in one go. 'Obviously I said no,' he told me, 'but, if I had agreed to sell it to him, I would have been very wary. It was a lot of money, though – it would have been hard to turn it down.'

'If I was to have got him the coke, I would have had to go over to Amsterdam to pick it up first.' So he had been smuggling drugs into the country as well as selling them at street level. 'And there's a good chance that he would have pulled a fast one. He would have said something along the lines of "I'll pay for three ounces and give you the rest of the money when I've got it." And he would have been trying to take me for a mug.'

Dutchy and the Jamaican ended up falling out. Dutchy was not someone who could be messed about with his money – not by anyone. 'I got on the phone, rang up four of my boys from the F-Side and they came over to teach him a lesson. They held him down and I cut two fingers off each of his hands – I'm not someone you can treat like a muppet and get away with it.'

As it happened, the Jamaican ended up nearly bleeding to death. He also went to the police. 'I don't get it!' Dutchy told me. 'If you're involved in selling drugs, then why go to the cops? There are a lot more grasses over here than there are in Holland – you'd never get that happening over there.' He was charged with attempted murder and sentenced to seven and a half years behind bars. As he was under 21, he served the first part of his sentence in Feltham Young Offenders' Institution. It was similar to the institution he had been in back in Holland, apart from the fact that he was allowed fewer visits and spent less time out of his cell. From there he went on to HMP Blundeston in Suffolk, HMP Wolds in Brough, East Yorkshire, and finally to HMP Everthorpe, also in East Yorkshire.

'Prison is prison. They were all pretty similar. The only thing I can say is that adult prison is a lot easier than YPs [young people's centre, a euphemism for a young offenders' institution] was,' he told me. When Dutchy got out, he moved back to Hull, but his girlfriend had been unwilling to wait the length of his sentence. He was now single again. 'I was on the hunt for fanny the minute I got out!' he laughed.

Within a few months, Dutchy had found a new girl to shack up with. They bought a house together on Newland Avenue and he went back to doing exactly what he had done before. Jail had taught him nothing. As far as he was concerned, crime was a way of life and a very profitable one at that.

'I had connections in the F-Side who could get me whatever I wanted,' he told me. He was still in regular contact with his old firm and he had even travelled down to London to join them in a clash against Arsenal. 'English firms are rough. The only thing the Dutch firms have on the English firms is their willingness to use guns and bombs.' I thought he could be exaggerating here but I have since researched the use of weapons by Dutch football hooligans and come across a number of instances in which guns and incendiary devices have been used. In 1989 Feyenoord's firm seriously injured a number of Ajax supporters by detonating two homemade nail bombs during a match. In 1999 there were reports of shots being fired by rioting Feyenoord fans. In August 2009 a man was shot dead as police and hooligans clashed at a Rotterdam beach party. Dutchy was telling the truth.

'They are more like gangs than firms nowadays. Using guns defeats the purpose of it, though. I've always liked having guns around me but I've never taken them to a football match.' It was his predilection for firearms that had eventually led to him receiving yet another jail sentence. The police came round to investigate an allegation that he had taxed a local drug dealer and uncovered two shotguns and an assault rifle in his house. 'The mad thing about it was I didn't even rob him with a gun – I used a machete!' he told me. 'Still, he testified against me and I went down for the robbery as well.' That was another seven years inside.

'Is that what you're in for now?' I asked him. 'Yeah,' he replied. 'Hopefully it'll be my last sentence.' I wondered whether that would be because he wasn't planning on doing any more crime or because he wasn't planning on getting caught. 'Nah – I really am going to pack it all in. I've been doing Summit and I'm going to go into affiliate marketing when I get out. It's taught me a trade – given me an honest way to live.'

Summit Media is a company that employs prisoners to carry out online marketing work. It pays between £10 and £35 a week and teaches its workers valuable skills that can greatly improve their employment prospects. Out of the 250 inmates Summit has taken on, only two have reoffended. It is one of the more successful rehabilitation initiatives that the prison system has put into place.

'I'm lucky in a way,' he went on. 'Some people go out and they have learned nothing. I couldn't have done half the things I can do on a computer if it wasn't for Summit.' So he had no plans to return to Holland, then? 'Nah, England's my home now. Besides, my missus has had a kid since I've come in here. I've got a child waiting for me out there.' So back to Hull, then. When finally released, he would have spent more of his adult life in prison than out.

'I had no excuse for getting into crime,' he told me. 'I came from a good family and, despite what people say, Slotervaart wasn't a bad place to grow up in. I just always craved excitement and breaking the law was my way of getting it.' Now that he was a bit older his attitudes appeared to be changing. 'Some of the things I did back then I wouldn't do nowadays – especially the football violence. Back then it was mostly fists with a few knives and bike chains – nowadays there's a lot more guns and bombs thrown into the mix. As I say, it's more like gang warfare.'

It seemed like Summit had come along just at the right time. He'd been looking for a means to earn a legitimate income and it had provided one for him. He recognised the fact that he couldn't go on selling drugs for ever and had been hanging on until a way out had presented itself. 'I've done two long sentences – I don't want to risk getting a third one!' he told me. 'I realised on this sentence that I would have to do something that wouldn't land me back in a cell.'

It was good to see an inmate who had realised the need for change, even if it was just to keep himself out of jail. He had led a colourful life and committed some horrific acts of violence but it was now time for him to leave the past behind. He didn't have long left to do and he would soon be back on the streets, ready to sink or swim. If he was unable to make it in the world of affiliate marketing, maybe he would lapse into his old ways again. For now, though, he had a new path to travel down – it was time to start afresh.

CHAPTER 23
NORTH HILL BILL

Jail is a lot easier if you have money. For those relying on the wage they are paid for their prison job, it is a meagre existence. For the drug dealers, loan sharks and taxmen, it is a life of relative comfort. Halfway into my sentence, I realised that, if I wanted to improve my day-to-day life, I was going to have to find a way of earning some 'burn'. I racked my brains – what could I do that the other inmates couldn't? A good number of them couldn't read or write. Up to 37 per cent of prisoners are functionally illiterate and only one in five is able to fill in an application form correctly. If I wanted to buy the more expensive items from the prison shop, I would have to make use of my English skills.

'Why don't you do poems for people?' my cellmate suggested. 'It's coming up to Valentine's Day – it'd be something different for them to send to the missus.' This was a good idea – some inmates were already making a healthy profit drawing pictures for cards. 'Put the word around,' I told him. 'Half a pack of burn for a poem.'

Jim was my first customer. He wanted me to write a poem to his solicitor girlfriend referencing Sherlock Holmes, Moriarti and Columbo. They were both fans of detective programmes – ironic given his hatred of the police. 'Make it a little bit horny as well,' he told me. 'Sex it up a bit.' Columbo and sex didn't exactly go hand in hand, but I did my best.

Before long, I was making a quarter of an ounce of tobacco every week. I was writing rhymes for all occasions – birthdays, anniversaries, even somebody's girlfriend coming out of rehab. 'Can you do one for my getaway driver?' one of my cellmate's friends asked me. Sure, I thought – why not?

Bill had been dating his getaway driver for the past few years. They were both amphetamine addicts and they were inseparable. 'You need to mention that she likes her whiz,' he told me. 'We both pin [inject] it – it's the best way of taking it.' I wasn't even aware that speed could be injected. 'Put "from North Hill Bill" at the end of it,' he instructed me. I was familiar with North Hill – it was a hall of residence for Leeds University students. 'Did you go to my uni, then?' I asked him. He grinned. 'Sort of. Well, the police think I did – they come to me whenever anything goes missing from there! That's how I got the nickname – they reckon I was always outside North Hill Court looking for bikes to steal.'

It was difficult working hypodermic needles and amphetamine addiction into a love poem but I gave it my best shot. Bill was enamoured with his driver – or 'Big S' as she was known. Crime was the second love of his life. He prided himself on his position as Leeds's biggest bike thief and was thought to be responsible for 56 thefts in a single month. As a result of the number of bikes going missing, investigative journalist Donal MacIntyre placed a tracking device in a top-brand bicycle and left it out as bait. The next thing Bill knew, he had a film crew in his face and a pair of cuffs around his wrists.

Bill was a success story in that he had managed to get himself off drugs while he was inside. He engaged with CARAT soon after arriving at the prison and they had helped him to overcome his addiction. 'I think it'll be harder to kick my bike addiction,' he grinned. 'I don't think I'll ever get rid of that one.' He admitted that he would never be able to hold down an honest job and had tried to find a crime that caused the least amount of harm to the victim. 'Losing a bike is an inconvenience,' he told me. 'That's all it is. It's bad but it's not as bad as having your house or your car broken into.'

For all his faults, Leeds's biggest bike thief was dedicated to his girlfriend through and through. 'It's hard being in here when she's out there,' he sighed. 'Things aren't going well for her and she needs me there.' I had heard on the grapevine that she was suffering from kidney damage from prolonged drug use and that she had just come out of hospital. It was good that he was willing to stand by her even though he had managed to kick his habit – although there was always the danger that she would drag him back into addiction when he got out.

Big S liked her poem. 'Cheers for that,' Bill told me. 'Here's your burn.' I stashed the tobacco down the front of my trousers. If the prison guards saw me being given items by other prisoners, they would assume I was selling drugs, so I had to be careful. 'I've not heard from her for a while, though,' he went on. 'I don't know what's going on with her.' This was a common dilemma: people's girlfriends would lose interest while the inmates were locked up. With no way of knowing what was going on while they were behind bars, they were left constantly waiting for news.

As the weeks went by, Bill became increasingly quiet and withdrawn. 'I wish she'd write to me,' he told me. 'I just want to know what's happening.' I felt bad for him. He was willing to stick with her through thick and thin but she was unwilling to reciprocate. 'Maybe she's just busy,' he reassured himself. 'Life goes on out there. We've got time to be writing letters every week here but she'll have things to do.' I nodded sympathetically.

Later that day, Bill came out of his cell looking close to tears. 'It's S,' he told me. 'I've just had my mate on the phone telling me she's been shagging another mush. What should I do?' There was only one thing for him to do: cut her off and find someone else. 'I can't leave her!' he whimpered. 'We've been through too much for that!'

The next time I saw Bill, his eyes were like saucers. 'Are you back on drugs?' I asked him. 'Yeah, I've been taking Subby,' he told me. 'And so what?' The break-up of his relationship had driven him back to his only means of coping. He took drugs to forget. It was easy to remain sober when life was going according to plan, but, now that the love of his life had betrayed him, he was a broken man. There was no point in trying.

It takes only a single lapse to renew an addict's taste for drugs. Within a few weeks, Bill was taking Subutex 24 hours a day and suffering withdrawal symptoms when he was unable to afford it. 'You sure you don't want to buy any Subby?' he would ask me. 'I need burn!' I told him that I didn't take drugs any more. 'Suit yourself,' he told me. 'It's good stuff, though!'

'Have you seen the state of Bill lately?' one of the inmates from Bill's estate asked me as we walked round the yard. 'Yeah,' I replied. 'He's gutted about that girl.' This inmate was in for punching a girl in the face – it's obvious what his response to the situation would have been. 'The other fella is his rival, too,' he told me. 'Leeds's second-biggest bike thief.' He had to be making this up. 'Nah, it's true,' he assured me. 'They're in competition.'

'Do you reckon you'll be back on the 'phet [amphetamine] when you get out?' I asked Bill a couple of days before he was due for release. 'To be honest, it's all I can think about at the moment,' he told me. At least he was being honest. 'Do you think you'll carry on seeing S?' I asked him. 'I don't know,' he answered. 'Maybe. I'd be better off not, though.' He seemed to love her far too much to break away from her. I had a feeling that he would forgive her – if she could prise herself away from Leeds's number two.

Bill was one of my close friends on the wing. He was surprisingly moralistic for a thief and seemed to have lost his path in life rather than deliberately chosen a life of crime. He was addicted to the buzz of stealing other people's possessions, yet at the same time he recognised that what he was doing was wrong and had made a conscious decision to stick to petty crime. 'No one likes their bike being robbed,' he told me, 'but it's better than doing tie-ups or mugging old ladies.' It was nice to meet someone who was morally lacking as opposed to totally immoral. I was sad to see him leave when he finally got out but pleased that he was a free man.

When I got out of prison, I did research on everyone I had been in prison with to see what the papers had to say about them. I typed Bill's name into Google and was met with an article about his latest spate of bike thefts. He had been arrested two months after getting out for stealing a £1,500 bicycle from a city-centre car park. Luckily for him he was able to avoid a custodial sentence and was given community service and a nine-month stint in rehab. He asked for 44 other offences to be taken into consideration.

On reading the article fully, I noticed that Bill had been driven to and from the car park by a female amphetamine addict, whose name began with the letter S. He hadn't had the heart to break up with her – just as I had predicted. They had a turbulent and unconventional relationship but they also had a lot in common. It would have been difficult for him to find another girl who was willing to be his getaway driver – they were bound together by crime and addiction. As far as he was concerned, she was the most compatible partner he was ever going to find – however unfaithful she may have been.

CHAPTER 24
MY STORY

Bill was from Seacroft, one of the largest council estates in Britain. I grew up in a stable, well-to-do family in a small, semi-rural town in the North of England. I was from a sheltered, middle-class background and had no real reason to have been peddling narcotics. So how did I end up selling drugs to a cop? Where had it all gone wrong?

My answer to this is that I did what thousands of people of my background were doing all over the UK, but just happened to get caught. Although what I did was stupid, it was far from uncommon. Although hard drugs such as crack and heroin are mainly confined to those at the poorer end of the social spectrum, certain drugs are prevalent among young people from all areas of society. Middle-class drug users often buy their drugs from middle-class drug dealers – I was filling a gap in the market.

When I was 15, I was playing football down at the

local park when an older boy showed me a small, brown lump of cannabis resin. I was in awe of it. To me, it represented the ultimate act of rebellion. We were warned over and over again about the dangers of drugs and now here I was beholding the very substance that I had been told to stay away from at all costs. 'Do you want to smoke some?' This was a question and a half. I wanted to say yes but something inside of me forbade me from doing so. 'Maybe next time,' I told him, not wanting to say no but at the same time worried about how it might affect me if I was to take it.

The following week I returned to the park determined to procure some cannabis to show off to my friends at school. I wasn't brave enough to smoke it but I was certainly brave enough to carry it about with me. I had no idea how much to buy or how much it cost. There was no way of even knowing if it was genuine marijuana, and there were all sorts of stories circulating about people being sold Oxo cubes and lumps of brown wax crayon. Still, if I couldn't tell the difference, my friends wouldn't be able to, either. I could always sell it on after I had finished displaying it – that way it didn't really matter how much I ended up paying for it.

'How much was that, then?' my friend Jeremy asked me. 'Erm, £15,' I told him. I was lying – I had only paid £10. 'You can buy it off me if you give me some.' That was him suckered. He was going to pay £5 over the odds *and* end up sharing it with me. It wouldn't be so bad trying it for the first time now that I was with someone

else who was in the same boat. 'It's a deal.' My first ever
drug deal. It was the start of a slippery slope.

'But how do we smoke it?' Ah. I had no idea how to
roll a joint. I didn't even have any rolling papers and I
had spent all my money on the weed. We ended up
heating it up and inhaling the fumes through the outer
casing of a pen. It didn't do much at all.

The next time I was at the park, I paid a few pounds
extra to buy the weed pre-rolled into spliffs. We decided
that we were going to smoke it during PE and planned it
for weeks on end. We had to do a cross-country run
through a patch of woodland at the side of the school
and thought that this would be the perfect place to get
high. It was out of sight of the teachers and we were
both extremely unfit and so no one would notice the
delay in our times. I choked my lungs out and didn't
experience any positive effects from it whatsoever. It
made me feel paranoid and slightly sick and that was
about it. From that day on, I decided that smoking weed
wasn't really for me. I liked the fact that it was illegal
but that was about it.

Cocaine was the next drug I decided to try. I was
round at my friend Boz's house listening to music at the
time. "'Ere, do you fancy doing a few lines of coke?' he
asked me. I was 17 – Boz was a good few years older
than I was and I had always secretly looked up to him.
If he was doing it, I figured that it must be the cool thing
to do. 'Sure,' I replied. 'Why not?'

He poured a small amount of white powder onto the
table and cut me a line. 'Here, this is how you do it,' he

told me, pulling out a rolled-up a £10 note and taking a snort. I quickly followed suit. Within a few seconds, my mouth had gone completely numb and I had a weird tingling sensation in the back of my head. I felt a sudden rush of energy and the music seemed louder and more intense. About 30 seconds later, I felt like shit. That was the problem with coke – it didn't last very long and it was very expensive for what it was. To carry on the high, you had to snort line after line and run the risk of getting yourself hooked.

So I had tried weed and coke and they were both pretty lame. Definitely not worth the money. I was beginning to think that drugs were severely overrated and people only took them because they were against the law. Time to leave them alone for a while and get on with my studying – I had exams coming up in a couple of weeks. After that I would be heading off to university, where I could experiment to my heart's content.

I left college with four mediocre A levels and an AS level. I could have done a lot better but it was enough to get me into my first choice of university, which was Leeds. Leeds had a reputation as a party city. To say there were a lot of drugs there would have been putting it mildly. You name it, there were people taking it. The only drugs that weren't in wide circulation were crack and heroin – everything else was openly available.

It was Mick, a Geordie media student, who first introduced me to ecstasy. I was visiting him in his home city of Newcastle during the end-of-term break and we were discussing our previous drug use. 'I've done it all,' he told me. 'I had to stop taking everything, though, 'cause I started seeing the Devil standing over me when I woke up in the morning.' This wasn't particularly encouraging. 'That was from the acid – most other things are OK if you take them in moderation.' I made a mental note never to touch acid. 'What drugs have you done?' he asked. I told him I had only ever taken weed and cocaine but that I was open-minded and would give most things a go. 'You need to try a pill,' he told me. 'You will never forget your first E.'

That night, Mick introduced me to Kate, a twentysomething dreadlocked hippie who was selling ecstasy to earn enough money to buy her own. I bought two pills for £10 – they looked like pink, grainy aspirin tablets. 'Just take half at first and see how it goes,' she advised me. 'They are pretty strong. Make sure you drink enough water with them as well.' This was the first time I had come face to face with a Class A drug dealer and she was not at all how I had expected her to be. She came across as kind and approachable – the type of person that you could speak to if you had a problem. 'Have a good night,' she told me. 'It'll be one to remember!'

I broke the pill in two, took half and waited. Nothing happened. How long was it meant to take before I started to feel any different? 'Be patient,' Mick advised. 'Let's go to a club and see if the music helps to bring it on.' This sounded like a good idea. Maybe I needed some type of stimulus for it to take effect. 'Some of my mates are in Cuba Cuba – do you want to go there?' Cuba Cuba is a rock club – not really my choice of music but it was better than sitting around in Mick's bedroom all night.

After a good half-hour inside the club I still felt exactly the same. 'What's actually meant to happen?' I whined. I was convinced I had been sold a duff pill. 'Just give it time.' How much more time did he want me to give it? It was a good two hours since I had taken it. 'You could always take the other half.' That was more like it – then we would know for sure whether I'd been sold a dud. 'Snort it up and it'll get into your bloodstream quicker.'

Five minutes later I began to feel intensely anxious, like the feeling you get when you are heading towards the top of a roller coaster. Finally, something was happening. My spine was tingling and my mouth was incredibly dry. I felt my pupils growing wider and my whole body relaxing as the tension began to melt away. Wow. I was starting to feel pretty damn good. My whole body felt ultra-sensitive and the hairs on my arms and legs were beginning to stand on end.

For the next few hours, I was in a state of complete euphoria. Rock had suddenly become my favourite type of music and I was telling anyone and everyone how great they were. 'Come on, we've got a taxi waiting – it's time to go home!' I wanted to stay and gibber incessantly about nothing. 'We can stay up and talk when we get home,' Mick assured me. Oh, OK, then. That sounded good. So long as it wasn't the end of the night and I could carry on talking.

Back at Mick's house, I talked relentlessly for a good ten minutes and then started to feel very uneasy. I felt drained and nauseous, and as if my brain had been put through a tumble drier. This isn't good, I thought to myself. I knew I had been pretty high and could sense I was due for some kind of comeuppance to balance things out. 'I think I need a bit of a lie-down,' I groaned. If taking ecstasy was such a happy, positive experience, why had Mick stopped taking it? Panic began to set in.

Next morning I woke up in a pool of my own puke. I didn't know where I was or how I'd got there. I tried to talk but my head was too scrambled to formulate any coherent words or phrases. I felt confused, depressed and sick. I was sick every ten minutes for the next four hours, and I could barely string a sentence together. Mick's mum and dad were sympathetic but at the same time clearly disapproving. He had told them what had happened and they were not best pleased. They eventually took me to hospital, where I was given an injection to stop me being sick. 'You probably got a dodgy pill,' the nurse told me. 'It's been cut with something nasty. Rat poison or something like that.' Thanks a lot, Kate. I thought hippies were supposed to be about peace and love but they were obviously more interested in ripping people off and leaving them violently sick.

So the ecstasy night was definitely not one to be repeated. Mick had presented a very one-sided view of its effects and he had neglected to mention all the other toxic chemicals crammed into the pills to bulk them out. It would be a while before I touched drugs again. So far I hadn't had a single positive experience on them.

The months went by and I slowly forgot how awful

my night in Newcastle had turned out. You would have thought I'd learned my lesson by then but, no, I was still an idiot. This time it was different, though – it was the first time things actually went well. I was visiting my friend Mike in Nottinghamshire and we were down at his local pub. His friend Tez was sitting next to us with a big stupid grin on his face talking hours and hours of irrelevant nonsense. I wondered what the hell was up with him. 'Don't mind Tez,' Mike explained. 'He's on the base tonight.' What the hell was base? I'd never even heard of it.

Base is high-class speed. It is purer than your average amphetamine and has had some of the impurities washed away. Tez seemed like he was having a good time on it. 'Have a little dab if you want,' he told me. Here I went again. I was about to take a drug that I knew relatively little about from somebody that I had only just met. 'Dip your finger in and eat the paste that sticks to it.' A few granules couldn't really do too much harm. I licked my finger and dipped it into the bag. It tasted like cat's piss. It really was foul.

Five minutes later, I began to get a warm, fuzzy sensation towards the front of my head. The saliva in my mouth had completely dried up but at the same time I couldn't stop talking. The music on the pub jukebox sounded amazing. It was as if every drumbeat were fuelling my high. I felt completely energised – as if I could have run around the room over and over again. And I'd only taken a minute amount. This stuff was certainly good value for money.

I spent the remainder of the night talking frantically and enthusiastically about things that I would have previously thought were boring. I had suddenly become passionately opinionated about everything. Mike was looking annoyed. He was stone-cold sober and clearly not enjoying himself. 'Let's go home,' he implored me. I didn't care where we were so long as I could carry on talking.

Back at Mike's, I must have talked for a good four hours straight. 'I'm going to bed,' he told me. He had finally had enough. What was I going to do now? I was still wide awake and bursting at the seams with drug-induced energy. The next few hours were very, very boring. I couldn't sleep but, at the same time, no one else was awake. When I did finally manage to get to sleep I kept waking up with a dry mouth. Still, the night had been a relative success in that I hadn't ended up in a puddle of my own vomit.

'If you want to buy some base to take home with you, the guy I get my weed off is selling it,' Mike told me. Seeing that I didn't know anyone in Leeds who could get hold of it, this would be the only way of getting any without making the trip back to Notts. 'Where does he live?' I asked. 'About five minutes from here,' he replied. I had a headache and felt as though I could sleep for days, but I was still vaguely capable of walking to the next estate and back. 'Let's do it,' I said.

The speed dealer was a 50-year-old man who looked as if he had taken far too much of his own produce. 'I've been up for the last three nights,' he boasted, as if it was a mark of the quality of the wares he had on offer. In reality, it was vaguely offputting. Was this the type of person I was going to end up as if I carried on taking drugs? 'Now this is probably stronger than the stuff you've had before in Leeds, so be careful with it.' I wasn't sure if he was genuinely concerned or trying to imply that it was good stuff so I would come back for more. It was probably cut with all sorts.

I paid £15 for a gram – not bad at all, considering that a tiny pinch of it had kept me awake until six o'clock in the morning. I got four sets of usage out of each gram and would buy another bag every time I went to Notts. Eventually, I managed to find a dealer in nearby Bradford, which was far more convenient. It meant that I could take it whenever I wanted. I knew that it was addictive, so I limited my intake – maybe once every two or three weeks at the very most.

By this time I was living in Hyde Park, a bohemian student area of Leeds where drugs were nothing out of the ordinary. There were wild ecstasy-fuelled parties most nights of the week and it was home to the type of people who had dreadlocks and called each other 'man'. Most of the local druggies took either MDMA or ketamine, which were easily available. By this stage, I was hanging around with a group consisting predominantly of drug users and I knew a few different dealers. There were times when two different dealers had stopped me on the street, trying to outdo each other in selling me the cheapest drugs.

One weekend, I was ringing around trying to get hold of

some speed but found myself unable to get through to anyone. 'I can't get any whiz,' I told my friends. 'I can get MDMA or ketamine, though – anyone up for trying either of them?' Nobody really fancied the ketamine. It had a bit of a rep. There were stories of people going insane from long-term use or taking too much in one go and lying paralysed for hours on end. MDMA it was, then.

MDMA is a brown, granulated powder. It is the one drug that tastes even worse than speed does. It is bitter and acidic and has an unpleasant, gritty consistency. I was wary about taking it as it was a form of ecstasy and I remembered what had happened the last time I'd taken an E. Here goes nothing, I thought as I licked the grit off the surface of the sealer bag. It was awful. I had to drink a whole can of Coke to get rid of the taste.

Within ten minutes, the lighting in the room had grown more intense and the surroundings had developed a warm orange glow to them. I felt calm but at the same time excited. I wasn't hyped up, as I had been on the speed or the ecstasy pill, but at the same time I felt as if something monumental was about to happen. My skin was hypersensitive and the fabric of my clothes felt amazing.

As soon as we left the house, the high really began to take effect. Everyday objects appeared strange and intriguing. Street lamps seemed hauntingly beautiful and old; decaying buildings were like classical works of art. A little voice in the back of my head kept telling me, 'You're safe. Everything's going to be OK.' This was the voice of the MDMA. I felt content, as if my life was exactly how it should be and everything was perfectly in order. This was by far the best drug I had ever taken.

The minute we entered the nightclub, I knew that we had come to the right place. The music sounded out of this world. It was repetitive, pumping dance music – the best thing to listen to when you are on any kind of drugs. I felt so happy. Even if I were to wake up semiconscious in a puddle of my own stomach acid, it would still be worth it for this.

The next day I woke up feeling perfectly fine. I was a bit tired, but that was to be expected. I'd also managed to get a perfect night's sleep. The only downside to the MDMA was its price. It was £35 a gram – fairly steep considering I was living on my student loan. I had taken a quarter of a gram out with me and it had lasted me the entire night. If I was to buy a gram, take a quarter and sell the other three quarters on for £10 each, I would be able to get high for a fiver a night.

'I'll tell you what,' my dealer told me. 'I'll sell you five grams for £100.' Then I could break each gram down into quarters and earn £20 a gram. I had a group of five friends who would buy a bag each every time we went out, bringing me in £25 profit a week. This was enough to pay the admission fee for whatever club we were going to and have enough left for a few drinks.

After every MDMA night, a couple of friends would come back to my house and sit about smoking weed. Had I started selling this as well, it could have been another convenient way of earning a few extra quid. I had a friend who was selling it and I could have easily struck up a deal with him whereby he gave me some £10 bags of weed to sell and I kept half of the profit. People were also asking if I could get hold of any ketamine. This cost £20 a gram and could be cut with scent-free talcum powder and sold at £15 for a half-gram bag.

I figured that, as long as I only sold to people I knew, there was no chance of getting found out. After all, I wasn't exactly Pablo Escobar – I was only making a few tenners here and there. Then came the fateful day I met 'Rachel'. Her name wasn't actually Rachel – she was an undercover cop.

I was recovering from a particularly nasty comedown when my friend Nitesh rang up asking if I could get any MDMA for a girl he had met. Apparently she had just moved to the city and didn't know where to get hold of any. I got her number off him and told him that I would see what I could do. After speaking to 'Rachel' on the phone, I decided she sounded like a legitimate drug user and agreed to sell her a £10 bag. The deal took place outside the Light shopping centre in Leeds city centre – a stupid place for a drug deal to take place, as it was completely covered by CCTV. Still, I figured that no one would be able to tell what I was passing over to her. 'Rachel' was dressed in a tracksuit and trying very hard to look like a chav. She seemed nervous but I assumed this was because she was worried about being spotted taking the drug bag. She passed me the money, I handed over the drugs and we headed off in separate directions.

The second time I sold to 'Rachel', she wanted to

meet outside the Co-op supermarket in Hyde Park. This was a few streets down from my house. This time she wanted a £20 bag. When I got to the Co-op the first thing I noticed was that she was dressed completely differently from when I'd first met her. She was now trying very hard to look like a student, and had a scarf and poncho on. This rang alarm bells. She had a bloke with her who looked far too old to be at uni. I was half expecting him to grab me and slap a pair of cuffs on, but he didn't. The deal went ahead without a hitch and at this point I assumed I was in the clear. What I didn't know was that the police don't arrest you straightaway: they try to get you to sell to them as many times as possible before striking.

Sure enough, a few weeks later I got a text on my phone asking if I could sort her out another £10 bag. By this stage, I was convinced she was the genuine article. Why else would I have been allowed to get away with the first two deals? I told her to meet me at the Co-op again. It would save me the effort of walking into town. Once again, the deal went ahead as planned. Maybe she had changed her style since the first time I met her and decided that tracksuits were no longer her thing. Whatever the reason for her sudden change of image, she was definitely the real McCoy.

The police waited for a good three months before pouncing. By that stage, I had finished at university and had just moved back in with my mum and dad. Knock, knock, knock. I was in bed at the time. The minute the door was open, three burly officers ran up the stairs and started shouting frantically in my face. 'Where are the drugs? Tell us where the drugs are! We know they're in here – you better tell us where they are!' I had absolutely no idea what was going on. I was half asleep and in a state of panic and confusion.

There were scales, sealer bags and a small amount of MDMA rather poorly hidden around my room. 'We'll tear the house apart unless you tell us where they are!' Shit. There was no way out of this one. That was my degree down the drain – there isn't much you can do with an English degree if you've got a record for selling Class A drugs as well. I showed the cops where the drugs were – it was the easiest way to get them to calm down.

'Right – I'm arresting you for the supply of Class A drugs. You don't have to say anything . . .' I'd seen it on TV but I had never expected to be on the receiving end of it. It was like something out of *The Bill*. They cuffed me up and led me out the front door into the back of a police wagon.

So here I was, about to enter the belly of the beast. I was sitting in a small, airless holding cell in the prison reception feeling absolutely terrified. To my left was an emaciated smackhead with a look of crazy desperation in his eyes and to my right was a large, heavily tattooed drug dealer. I was the only one in a suit – everyone else was in a tracksuit. 'What are you, some kind of solicitor?' the smackhead asked me. I stood out like a sore thumb.

'Here's your ID card – from now on, you are prisoner

number WK5633. You're going to be spending the next few days on the induction wing so you can learn the ropes.' The receptionist signalled to a giant of a prison screw, who promptly unlocked the gate and ushered me through.

The induction wing was fairly quiet. There were only six other prisoners on there at the time. There were two coke dealers, a heroin dealer, a fraudster, a murderer and my cellmate Barry, who was in for selling coke and MDMA. Barry had been in his final year at university and was devastated that he was to miss out on completing his degree. He had sold drugs to a copper, been arrested for it and then foolishly sold to the same cop again while out on bail. Still, he was fairly pleasant company. It was his first time in jail and he was in a similar situation to mine. He was from a poor background and had been selling drugs to fund himself through university. Growing up in Chapeltown, he had witnessed his peers getting into all kinds of trouble over drugs and maintained a strict policy of selling only to other students, as they would be unlikely to burst into his house with a gun.

Barry was fairly relaxed and easygoing. He seemed determined to make the best of a bad situation and he would spend his time doing press-ups and reading academic textbooks. 'I want to come out of here smarter and stronger,' he told me. I wondered what life would be like on the main wing. If it was as chilled out as the induction wing I would be laughing. But what if they put me in a cell with a murderer or a rapist? I didn't even know which unit I would be on: we were due to find that out the following morning. I hoped it wasn't the dreaded C Unit. It was nearly as bad as the Notorious E Unit, and I didn't really fancy my chances there. I would just have to wait and see.

'Get your things. You're off to C Unit.' Just my luck. Oh, well, it couldn't be that bad, surely. 'Nah – it's OK, really,' the guard reassured me. 'There's just a lot of drugs there and it's got a bit of a gang problem at the moment.' Oh, great. I was heading into the middle of some kind of gang war – and I couldn't fight my way out of a paper bag.

C Unit was a lot noisier than the induction wing. It was also full of smackheads. Drug-addled bodies filled the landings, wide-eyed and stick thin. It was like a scene from *Dawn of the Dead*. I was the odd one out – the only one who didn't have any tattoos for one thing. The majority of the wing were covered in them from head to toe. As I walked up the stairs to my cell, I felt a tight knot of fear forming in the pit of my stomach. I just hoped that my cellmate was OK. If he was stealing my belongings and selling them for smack every two minutes, the next year was going to be a nightmare.

My cellmate turned out to be an Irish Gypsy, in for selling coke and firearm possession. In fact, he was quite a nice guy – he looked after me and made sure that I was OK during my first few weeks inside. He was well respected by his fellow inmates and appeared to have a fair bit of clout on the wing. 'If anyone gives you any trouble, you come and see me,' he told me. 'No one will say boo to you, though. Just keep your head down and you'll be OK.'

The first time I ventured outside the cell, I was on edge the whole time. There were a few familiar faces there – I recognised one of the black inmates from the local news. He had stabbed another man to death a few weeks earlier. Anthony Morley was another wing celebrity. He had stabbed his gay lover in the throat, cut off chunks of his flesh, seasoned them with herbs, fried them in olive oil and eaten them. I was right to be wary – it was like a melting pot of various ne'er-do-wells and psychopaths.

After a while, I began to get used to the idea that I was living around volatile and dangerous people. It became nothing out of the ordinary. Although there were some people in there who had done horrific things on the outside, jail was for the most part fairly trouble-free. There was the odd violent incident and I witnessed a few things I never thought I would have to see, but mainly it was just boring. I watched telly, played computer games, read books and talked to people about the details of their crimes.

Soon I had become just another con. I had shaved my head, started using words like 'shiv' and 'screw' in general conversation and assimilated myself into prison culture. The only difference between me and the other prisoners was my accent. I spoke 'posh'. 'You going back to your mansion when you get out, Lord Snooty?' the other prisoners joked. This was an integral part of prison culture – 'working' each other. But making constant jokes at each other's expense got a little wearing after a while. Lee, an inmate with a long, pointed nose, was repeatedly referred to as Swordfish, and another prisoner who was in for strangling his wife was predictably labelled the Boston Strangler. These jokes were used again and again to the point where they were no longer in the least bit funny.

I had eight different cellmates during my time inside – Barry (MDMA and coke dealer), Danny (Gypsy coke dealer), Craig (assault), Tendai (benefit fraud), Mark (assault), Hanksy (stabbed his ex-girlfriend), Ibrahim (crack and heroin dealer) and Max (murder). I had assumed that I would share a cell with the same person for the duration of my stay, but some inmates were released and others moved around the prison for various reasons. This caused a constant sense of uncertainty – there was always the nagging question of whom you would have to share with next.

Jail changed the way in which I looked at human beings. It made me see the things that they were capable of. I had always assumed that most people tried to be moralistic but some were unable to do so. The people I met inside painted a very different picture – there was a sizeable chunk of society that just didn't care. If somebody got hurt, good, just so long as it wasn't them. Some inmates had found ways of justifying their crimes to themselves but the majority were completely unconcerned with such things. They recognised that what they were doing was wrong and carried on doing it anyway.

On the day of my release, I stood at the prison gates wondering what type of world I was heading out into. I had met murderers, gangsters, drug addicts and paedophiles – an eclectic combination of the worst of the worst. I had heard endless stories about shootings, stabbings, kidnaps and robberies and I had seen stab marks, gunshot scars and even axe wounds.

As the gates slid open, I breathed a sigh of relief. I had survived – it was back to normality. But I was now very aware that it was a normality I had to share with the kind of people I had spent the last year with. They were gone but not forgotten. Just as every town and city has its doctors, lawyers and accountants, every council estate has its burglars, TWOCers, muggers and dealers. Those who live in the shadows. Those for whom crime is part of everyday life.

When I got home from prison, I went on the Internet and tried to find out whether what I'd heard during my time inside was true. I looked up gun crime in Hull – I wanted to see if Bolty was telling the truth. I discovered a lengthy catalogue of offences and noticed a recurring theme: every time there was a shooting, the police made a point of assuring the public that it was a 'one-off incident' and that gun crime was 'rare' in the city. They were either making good use of the fact that it was not a city traditionally associated with firearms or they were living in cloud cuckoo land.

April 2008 – a shot is fired through the window of a house in East Hull.

July 2008 – a convicted drug dealer is shot and killed at a house on Westerdale Road, East Hull.

July 2008 – a man is shot with a sawn-off shotgun at

a house on Wells Street, west Hull. A search of the assailant's house reveals a revolver, a flare gun, knuckle-dusters, a crossbow and a canister of CS gas.

January 2009 – a 20-year-old man is shot in the stomach outside Hull's KC Stadium.

January 2009 – a man is robbed at gunpoint in his own home in nearby Beverley. He has £50 and a laptop stolen.

February 2009 – two men are arrested in connection with a grenade found in north Hull.

February 2009 – a 22-year-old man is arrested on suspicion of supplying a firearm.

April 2009 – a man is charged with firearm possession after a witness claims to have seen him wielding a gun on Anlaby Road, west Hull.

November 2009 – a gun is found during raids at Craven Park market in east Hull.

And so it went on.

The next thing I looked up was gun crime involving the travellers. I found that shootouts between rival travelling families appear to be a regular occurrence in the Republic of Ireland.

April 2008 – a feud between two travelling families in Waterford ends in the fatal shooting of 21-year-old Martin Ward.

August 2008 – a 14-year-old boy is shot in Waterford as part of the same feud.

August 2008 – a 16-year-old Waterford traveller girl is shot in the legs, stomach and side. It is announced that family feuds in the city have cost the local police a total of £400,000.

August 2008 – 11 men are arrested for their part in a traveller family feud on the Dalton Park estate in Mullingar. One faces charges under the Firearms and Offensive Weapons Act.

August 2009 – a traveller is arrested in Tralee for wielding a shotgun during a confrontation with a rival family.

August 2009 – a man suffers facial injuries after shots are fired at a travelling site in Dungarvan.

October 2009 – a man is arrested in possession of a shotgun in Tralee. He is thought to be involved in a traveller family feud.

October 2009 – an explosive device is found at a house in Edgeworthstown. The owner of the house is suspected to be involved in a prolonged feud with a rival travelling family.

All these feuds received extensive media coverage, but such events barely make the papers in the UK – although there have been a number of major feuds in recent years that have lead to shootings, stabbings and even murders.

February 2008 – a Belfast man is hacked to death with a machete in front of his pregnant wife and children. The killing is thought to be linked to a dispute between rival travelling families.

October 2008 – the last remaining official Gypsy encampment in Glasgow is shut down. Locals blame a violent family feud, resulting in the shooting of a 16-year-old boy.

February 2009 – shots are fired into the house of a

settled traveller in West Belfast. It is allegedly related to the machete killing of the previous year.

March 2009 – a ten-year-old is arrested in connection with the shooting of an eight-year-old boy at a travellers' site in South Tyneside.

August 2009 – a 17-year-old boy and a 55-year-old grandmother are charged with attempted murder after firing shots into a caravan in West Belfast. It is rumoured to be the result of an ongoing feud between two groups of travellers.

Clearly there are problems in our country that are severely downplayed by the authorities. The last thing I looked up was the use of violence and torture during robberies. I was disturbed by Willy's accounts of what went on during his tie-ups and wanted to see just how commonplace such events were. It seemed that they were a regular occurrence.

February 2009 – a man is left with a fractured eye socket and a broken jaw after a robbery at a house in Middleton.

March 2009 – a Lancashire man is beaten with a crowbar and robbed in his own home.

May 2009 – a man is tortured with boiling water during a robbery at a house in Hyde.

June 2009 – an 88-year-old woman has her leg broken in two places by thieves at her West Sussex home.

June 2009 – a couple are dragged out of bed, kicked and punched during a robbery in Liverpool.

June 2009 – a man is punched in the face and robbed at gunpoint at a house in Walthamstow, East London.

July 2009 – a man is shot with a Taser gun during a robbery at a house in Walsall.

July 2009 – a Wigan man is attacked and robbed in his own home. He is hit with baseball bats and cut with machetes in front of his wife and baby.

August 2009 – a pair are jailed for stabbing a woman in the stomach during a robbery at a house in Weymouth.

September 2009 – a woman is seriously assaulted and robbed at a flat in north London. The attacker sets fire to her property before leaving.

I wrote this book to show how sick and brutal society can be. For such an affluent island, Britain has a disturbingly large amount of violent crime. It is also a place where the rich and the poor lead very different lives. I had no idea there was gun crime in seemingly mundane places like Hull. If someone had told me there were Gypsies with MAC-10s and bulletproof vests I simply wouldn't have believed them. There is a hidden world that operates in parallel to our own. A world bound by an unbreakable code of silence. A world where to be a grass is worse than to be a paedophile or rapist.

GLOSSARY OF JAIL SLANG

5-0/busies/fuzz/filth/plodders – police
8 mil – an 8 milligram Subutex tablet
Aggy – aggravated burglary
Armed blag – an armed robbery
Bang-up – the time in which the inmates are locked behind their cell doors
Banger – a gang member
Beast/monster/nonce – a sex offender
Benzo – benzodiazepine, an anti-anxiety drug
Bewer/fish/fruit/split-arse – a woman
Blicks – an automatic weapon
Block/seg – the segregation unit
Boot – a heroin pipe
Borer – a knife
Braying – hitting
Bricks/pen – prison
Brown/B/brandy/dirty/gear/nasty – heroin
Burg – a burglary

Burn – tobacco

Canteen – the prison shop

Cat – a drug addict

Catting – craving (see also *fiending*)

Cheeking – storing drugs between the buttocks

Chor – steal

Cloggy – a night watchman

Cowey – a stash of money

Crank/ding/dingy – an undesirable person

Creeper/sneak-thief – the act of sneaking into a person's house while they are still in it and stealing their property

Debt-head – someone who is always in debt

Double bubble – a system whereby if you lend something to someone they expect twice as much back

Digging/pinning – injecting

Doing the rattle – coming off heroin

Dry snitching – informing on someone by talking loudly about their activities or by spreading rumours about what they are doing

Face – a well-known criminal

Fax/script – a letter

Fiending – craving (see also *catting*)

Firm – a gang

Firm up – to form a gang

Food/work – hard drugs

Fraggle – a derogatory term for a physically weak inmate

Gat/piece/shooter/skeng/strally/strap/trigger/leng/mash – a gun

Gipton rolex/Runcorn rolex/Peckham rolex – an electronic leg tag

Granny-basher – an inmate who has committed an offence against the elderly

Green goblin/Shrek juice – methadone
Graft – obtain by illegal means
Grass – an informer
Hooch – a homemade alcoholic beverage made by fermenting oranges
Hoolie bird – a girl who gains sexual pleasure from sleeping with hooligans
Hot/on top – suspicious
IPP – initialism for an indeterminate sentence given in the *i*nterest of *p*ublic *p*rotection
Joey – a runner
Juck – stab
Kanga/screw/Scooby – a prison guard
Laptopping – the act of stealing laptops
Lifed off – given a life sentence
Line – a piece of fabric that is used to lower items out of the window and swing them from cell to cell
L plates – a life sentence
Naughty – anything that is particularly violent or extreme
Numbers/VP – the vulnerable prisoner wing
Pad – a cell
Pad rushing – the act of storming into another inmate's cell in order to steal his belongings. This is normally done in a group of around five or six people
Pad spin – a cell search
'Phet – speed
Pin – a heroin needle
Plugging – hiding something in the rectum
Raise – an illegal way of earning money
Roid rage – anger problems caused by excessive use of steroids
Rottle – *release on temporary licence*

Soap bar – low-quality hash
Screwboy – an inmate who is overfamiliar with the prison guards
Screwess – a female prison guard
Shank/shiv – a homemade knife
Shitting up – smearing the walls of a cell with faeces
Shot – sell
Slashing up – self-harming
Spinner – the guard whose duty it is to perform cell searches
Sleeper – a sleeping tablet
Straightener – an organised fist-fight used to settle a dispute
Stress-head – someone who stresses about every aspect of prison life
Subby – Subutex, a heroin substitute
Subby-head/Subby monster – a Subutex addict
Swill – to throw a mixture of sugar and boiling water into another inmate's face; the sugar sticks to their skin and burns it off
Tie-up – the act of tying someone up in their own home to rob them
TWOC – a stolen car (acronym for *t*aking *w*ithout *o*wner's *c*onsent)
TWOC slag – a girl who sleeps with joy riders
Tapping – begging
Tax – to rob
Taxman – someone who makes a living from robbing criminals
Teck – a mobile phone
Trammy (tramadol) – a codeine-based pain killer